# CRYSTAL
# JEWELRY
# CREATIONS

CREATE
YOUR STYLE
with SWAROVSKI ELEMENTS

# CRYSTAL JEWELRY CREATIONS

DOROTHY WOOD

Over **30** stunning and
original projects featuring
sparkling crystal beads

David and Charles

A DAVID & CHARLES BOOK
Copyright © David & Charles Limited 2010

David & Charles is an F+W Media Inc. company
4700 East Galbraith Road, Cincinnati, OH 45236

First published in the UK and US in 2010

Text and designs copyright © Dorothy Wood 2010
Photography on pages 89–91 copyright © Swarovski 2010

A catalogue record for this book is available
from the British Library.

ISBN-13: 978-0-7153-3633-5 paperback
ISBN-10: 0-7153-3633-9 paperback

Printed in China by RR Donnelley
for David & Charles
Brunel House, Newton Abbot, Devon

Publisher  Alison Myer
Acquisitions Editor  Jennifer Fox-Proverbs
Assistant Editor  Juliet Lines
Project Editor  Ame Verso
Design Manager  Sarah Clark
Photographers  Sian Irvine and Ally Stuart
Production Controller  Kelly Smith
Prepress  Jodie Culpin

David & Charles publish high quality books on a wide
range of subjects. For more great book ideas visit:
**www.rucraft.co.uk**

# CONTENTS

# *introducing*
# JEWELLERY CREATIONS *with* SWAROVSKI ELEMENTS

Swarovski have been synonymous with class and elegance ever since the late 19th century when Daniel Swarovski pioneered his innovative cutting machine, which made Swarovski crystals sparkle and shine like diamonds. Since then the company he founded has consistently widened the parameters for crystal as a creative material and in recent years has developed SWAROVSKI ELEMENTS as the ultimate cut crystal for jewellery design.

This book showcases over 30 stunning designs that feature some of the gorgeous crystals from the SWAROVSKI ELEMENTS range. As the crystals are available in a variety of styles, from Beads to Flat Backs, with a wide range of colours and finishes, there was no shortage of choice when it came to creating the designs. By way of inspiration the book is divided into eight chapters each with its own distinctive colourway, and titles such as Soft and Pretty, Dark and Dangerous and Tutti Frutti, give some indication of the delights within.

As well as having a distinct colour theme, each chapter also features a technique, perhaps wirework or a bead stitch, and so whether you are a beginner or experienced beader, there is plenty to inspire and whet your appetite. One design in every chapter is clearly illustrated with stunning step-by-step photographs and there is a packed techniques section showing all the skills you will need to complete the other projects.

Each chapter has four different items of jewellery, including necklaces, bracelets, rings and other accessories, all exquisitely photographed, and although some designs use only SWAROVSKI ELEMENTS and Swarovski Crystal Pearls, others include a variety of beads from tiny rocailles to big, bold beads. Sourced from a variety of bead shops listed on page 125, these beads may be difficult to match exactly but by choosing similar Swarovski Beads you will be able to create your own beautiful and totally unique pieces.

# CREATE YOUR STYLE *with* SWAROVSKI ELEMENTS

With the company's long history of collaboration with the world's leading designers and couturiers, Swarovski understands the creative process involved in using crystal to bring highly individual visions to life. Through the CREATE YOUR STYLE with SWAROVSKI ELEMENTS initiative, the company shares this exciting process with fashion-forward individuals, opening up a new world of personal expression through crystal. CREATE YOUR STYLE focuses on the endless possibilities offered by SWAROVSKI ELEMENTS, the extensive collections of Swarovski Beads, Pendants, Flat Backs, to name a few, in seemingly endless different shapes, sizes, colours and effects. These sparkling elements can be threaded, sewn or glued, mixed and mingled together or combined with the widest choice of materials – from fabric, leather and felt to wood and paper. The SWAROVSKI ELEMENTS product collection is updated and enhanced twice a year with new colours and products, keeping one step ahead of worldwide trends in fashion, style and design.

The product brand is known particularly for its highly directional range of crystal colours, seductive, innovative and emotive. SWAROVSKI ELEMENTS is constantly developing and expanding its refined colour palette, led by its expert in-house trend research team, providing a sense of continual anticipation and excitement, and colours to fit all styles, moods and occasions. Swarovski has continually pushed boundaries of innovation and crystal creativity. Today, SWAROVSKI ELEMENTS, unrivalled in quality, precision and consistency and known worldwide for its exceptional brilliance and irresistible range of colours and textures, is the ultimate luxury ingredient in fashion, jewellery, objects and lifestyle accessories. Through the CREATE YOUR STYLE with SWAROVSKI ELEMENTS initiative, these crystal elements that provide a continual source of inspiration and innovation to leading professionals,designers, jewellers and artisans around the globe, are available to individual customers everywhere, bringing a touch of couture luxury to personal creations.

## Personal Elegance

Taking the concept of individuality and self-expression to a new dimension, the CREATE YOUR STYLE with SWAROVSKI ELEMENTS initiative leads the way forward into a new era of glamorous, personalised creativity and brings a fresh sophisticated elegance to the whole process of 'personal design'. The art of creating your own customised crystal style, either from scratch or by transforming an existing design, has grown to be an integral element of luxury today, part of a far-reaching, global trend – a cultural fusion of vintage, couture and street-style.

# SOFT *and* PRETTY

The soft textures of silky rattail, organza ribbon, waxed cord and delicate mesh ribbon make a wonderful foil for pretty pastel shades of SWAROVSKI ELEMENTS. Inspired by memories of skipping through flower-filled meadows as a child, these pieces of jewellery, each featuring flowers or insects, encapsulate that delicate ethereal quality.

## *flora* NECKLACE

A summer wedding or May ball would be the ideal occasion to wear this fabulous necklace and, as you don't want anything too fussy against such an ornate design, a simple strapless or low-cut gown would show it off beautifully. The necklace's colours also make it ideal for a more casual garden party. The design incorporates Fancy Stones that have no holes, but that come with their own specially designed settings. The 'beadling' flowers are easy to make using a simple weaving technique and then the necklace is sewn together with wire to create the shape, embellished with delightful Crystal Pearls and finished with organza ribbon.

## YOU WILL NEED

- Pink organza ribbon, 2m (2¼yd) of 15mm (⅝in)
- Square Setting in antique silver, 12mm
- Oval Setting in antique silver, 18 x 13mm
- Round Setting in antique silver, 8mm
- Silver-plated wire, 0.315mm (30swg) and 0.6mm (24swg)
- 2 silver-plated domed bead sieves, 10mm
- 3 triangle bails
- Basic tool kit (see pages 94–95)

SWAROVSKI ELEMENTS

– XILION Bead 5328 – Violet Opal (389) 3mm x 50; Rose
   Alabaster (293) 3mm x 50; Rose Water Opal (395) 3mm x 50;
   White Opal (234) 3mm x 50; Light Amethyst (212) 3mm x 68;
   Light Rose (223) 3mm x 68

– Square Fancy Stone 4470 – Rose Alabaster (293) 12mm x 4

– Oval Fancy Stone 4120 – Light Rose (223) 18 x 13mm x 3

– Round Stone XILION Chaton 1028 – Vintage Rose (319) 8mm x 5

– Crystal Pearl 5810 – Powder Rose Pearl (352) 5mm x 18

– Crystal Button 3015 – Light Amethyst M (212) 10mm x 5

– Briolette Pendant 6010 – Light Rose (223) 11 x 5.5mm x 3

1 Mix the Light Amethyst XILION Beads (5328 3mm 212) and
Light Rose XILION Beads (5328 3mm 223) (A) on a beading
mat and in a separate pile mix the Rose Alabaster XILION Beads
(5328 3mm 293) and White Opal XILION Beads (5328 3mm 234)
(B). Pick up three A XILION Beads on a 50cm (20in) length of
0.315mm (30swg) wire and drop down to the middle. Take one
end back through the last two XILION Beads and pull up to
make a triangle shape of Swarovski Beads for the top of a petal.

2 Pick up one A, one B and one A on one wire and take the
other end through these Swarovski Beads in the opposite
direction. On the next row pick up one A, two B and one A
then feed the other wire through as before.

3 Continue adding rows with one A on
each side and the centre Swarovski
Beads as follows: work three rows with
three Bs in the middle and then a row
with two Bs and a last row with one B
in the middle. Twist the wires together
at the bottom of the petal a couple of
times to secure the Swarovski Beads.

4 Make another nine petals. Arrange five petals in a flower shape. Pick up a Light Amethyst Crystal Button (3015 10mm M 212) on two strands of fine wire and feed the tails through the middle of the petals then twist all the wires together under the petals. Feed the wires through the centre of the bead sieve. Secure the wires by splitting the bundle and feeding back through the sieve as neatly as possible and trim. Make another flower in the same way.

5 Set the Fancy Stones (4470 12mm 293) (4120 18 x 13mm 223) into their Settings by holding the Fancy Stone in position and pressing down on the metal lugs with the side of flat-nose pliers or a similar solid surface (see page 104).

6 Lay the SWAROVSKI ELEMENTS and the flowers face down on the work surface or a beading mat to create the shape of the necklace following the diagram on page 127.

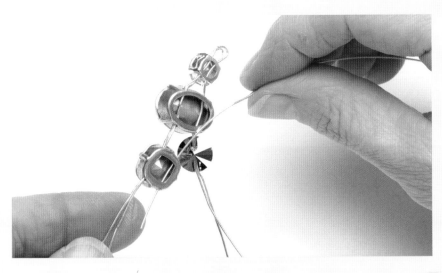

7 Pick up one of the XILION Chatons (1028 8mm 319) from the top outer corners and feed the tails of a 1m (1yd) length of 0.6mm (24swg) wire through the holes in the Setting. Feed a second wire through in the same direction. Pull the wires through until there is a small loop on one side. Following the diagram on page 127, begin to add Fancy Stones and Buttons to create the shape of the necklace. Pass one wire through each hole in the settings to begin with and then build up the shape, taking wires across from one shape to the other. Leave gaps between some of the Chatons and Fancy Stones so that you can add clusters of pearls later.

Try to avoid making too many kinks in the wire as you thread the pieces together so that the back looks as neat as possible.

8 Feed the wires through the holes in the bead sieve to attach the flower. Add four more Fancy Stones and a Button following the diagram. Turn the beaded piece over from time to time to check that the Beads are lying together attractively and adjust if required.

9 Create the other side of the necklace as far as the beaded flower. Join the sides together through the Square Fancy Stone (4470 12mm 293) marked with an asterisk on the diagram on page 127. If there are too many pieces of wire, trim any excess wire neatly and continue with the remaining wires. Loop one or two wires through the last XILION Chaton (1028 8mm 319) at the bottom to make a loop again.

10 Trim off any excess wires and tuck in neatly. Lay the beaded piece face up and decide where to add pearls. Pick up a Crystal Pearl (5810 5mm 352) on fine wire and drop down to the middle. Wrap the wires around the heavier wire between the Fancy Stones. Pick up another Crystal Pearl and secure again. Continue adding clusters of Crystal Pearls until all the gaps are filled.

11 Fit a triangle bail through the bottom loop on the beaded piece. Attach a light rose Briolette Pendant (6010 11 x 5.5mm 223). Attach the other Briolette Pendants on the side of the beaded piece so that they hang attractively.

12 Cut the organza ribbon in two and then fold each length in half. Feel the ribbon through the loops at the top of the beaded piece and then take the tails through the ribbon loop. Pull up to secure. Hold the necklace at the height you want to wear it and then tie the ribbons at the back of your neck.

# *more...*
# SOFT *and* PRETTY

Delicate pastels, pinks, lilac and green are undoubtedly pretty colours for jewellery inspired by summer meadows, and these delightful designs have a gentle feel in keeping with swaying grass and flitting insects. The addition of a textile to each piece, either cord or a mesh ribbon, has created wonderfully soft and pretty items.

**CORDIAL CHARM ...**
*bracelet*

**BUTTERFLY KISSES ...**
*earrings*

**GLISTENING DEMOISELLE ...**
*hair clip*

# *cordial* CHARM

Soft and silky rattail, usually sold to hang
Pendants or to make simple knotted necklaces,
makes a beautiful rope that can be incorporated
into jewellery designs and the gorgeous sheen of the
rattail looks even better when twisted. The cut ends
can be hidden inside a bell cone end and the loop
end is easily secured with a jump ring (see pages
98 and 102). Choose colours of rattail that match
the gorgeous Crystal Flower Pendants and
this simple knotted bracelet can be created
in next to no time. To add a little extra
sparkle and contrast to lift the design,
use a couple of round crystals in
pale green as bead dangles using
decorative headpins (see page
100). For the materials list
and instructions, turn to
page 114.

# BUTTERFLY *kisses*

Waxed cord is available in a myriad of pretty colours and is one of the most popular threading materials for casual jewellery, but as this delightful set of earrings shows it can be incorporated into more formal designs too. The secret is finding the right shade of cord for the crystals so that the two elements pull together as one. Waxed cord comes in a range of thicknesses – you will need a fine cord for this design so that several strands will fit through the hole in the Butterfly Pendants. The wrapping technique, which is ideal for this fine cord, creates a neat tube that adds an unusual design feature to the earrings and also hides all the raw ends. Add earring wires and some pretty crystal dangles and they're done. For the materials list and instructions, turn to page 118.

## *glistening* DEMOISELLE

A perennial favourite, the dragonfly is such a delightful shape to recreate in Swarovski Beads, with its perfectly balanced wings, abdomen and elegant tail. This gorgeous hair clip design is so realistic it will look like a real dragonfly has flown down and landed on the wearer's hair. The wings are sculpted quite simply from craft wire and enclosed in fine tubular mesh ribbon and then the body of the dragonfly is created with a coiled string of silver beads and tiny SWAROVSKI ELEMENTS. The eyes of the dragonfly are made from a Modular Bead, an unusually shaped crystal with wrapped wire in the middle, and the tail is formed from a line of graduated crystals ranging from 2–7mm. For the materials list and instructions, turn to page 121.

# BRIGHT
# *and* BOLD

Red, pink and orange are harmonious colours from the warm side of the colour wheel but that doesn't mean that they make boring jewellery. Slight adjustments in tone when choosing the beads and the finished pieces come to life. All these designs use a right-angle weave technique (see page 109) combined with Swarovski XILION Beads.

## *rocky road* BANGLE

When thinking bright and bold it is easy to think of solid blocks of colour but this bangle uses a whole range of subtle shades of Swarovski XILION Beads to stunning effect. Fuchsia and Rose are the main colours in the bangle with Light Peach for contrast and the addition of a few bright orange crystals adding highlights and extra impact. Right-angle weave, especially with the extra pearlized seed beads in each ring, is not strong enough to hold the circular shape of the bangle but by sewing cross struts using the orange pearlized seed beads, the structure becomes much stronger.

## YOU WILL NEED

- Seed beads, size 9 (2.6mm), 15g each of pale orange pearlized and pale red pearlized
- Fireline beading thread in smoke, size D
- Beading glue
- Basic tool kit (see pages 94–95)

SWAROVSKI ELEMENTS

- XILION Bead 5328 – Fuchsia (243) 6mm x 45, Rose (209) 6mm x 45, Light Peach (362) 6mm x 32, Fire Opal (237) 6mm x 6, Sun (248) 6mm x 6

*Work the right-angle weave mainly in Fuchsia and Rose, adding Light Peach for contrast and the brighter oranges as highlights.*

1 Mix the Fuchsia XILION Beads (5328 6mm 243) and Rose XILION Beads (5328 6mm 209) on a beading mat, with the other XILION Bead colours and the pale red pearlized seed beads in separate piles. On a 2m (2¼yd) length of thread pick up a pale red pearlized seed bead and a XILION Bead from the mixed pile four times then go back through the beads and pull up to make a circle. Take the needle through two seed beads and three XILION Beads so that the tail and working thread emerge at opposite sides.

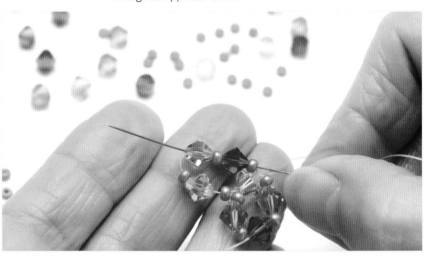

2 To work the right-angle weave pick up a seed bead and a XILION Bead three times and then another seed bead. Take the needle through the top XILION Bead from the previous circle and then back through two seeds and two XILION Beads to emerge at the top of the bead chain again.

3 Continue adding circles of beads to make a right-angle weave chain with 21 rings (see page 109). With each new ring you will circle round in the opposite direction to the previous ring. You can adjust the length of the bracelet at this stage – this size of bracelet fits a 7–7½ (S–M) glove size.

4 To work a second row next to the first take the needle through a seed bead and a XILION Bead to bring the thread out under a side XILION Bead. Pick up a seed bead and a XILION Bead three times and then another seed bead. Take the needle through the side XILION Bead again and through the circle beads only, to emerge at the bottom XILION Bead.

5 For the next circle pick up a seed bead, a XILION, a seed bead, a XILION and a seed bead. Take the needle through the side XILION on the second circle down from the previous row. Pick up a seed bead and then continue through the beads in the circle to come out at the bottom XILION again.

6 With the additional seed beads in this right-angle weave you need to remember to add the 'missing' seed beads as you circle round. There should be four seed beads between the XILION Beads in the centre of the two rows. Work down the row adding only enough beads to complete each circle, using XILION Beads and seed beads from previous circles as needed.

Pull the thread tight after adding each single XILION Bead to encourage the bracelet to curve.

7 Once you have completed two rows of 21 circles, work back up to join the two rows to make a triangle cross-section. On this row don't add any seed beads, only XILION Beads – this causes the bangle to curve. Pass the needle through the last circle until it emerges from the side bead then pick up a XILION Bead and go through the XILION Bead on the opposite side. Pick up another XILION Bead and pass through the other side bead then pull the thread taut to create the triangle shape.

8 Pass the needle through all four XILION Beads again in the circle just formed to come out at the last XILION added again. On the next and subsequent circles of right-angle weave only add one XILION as you pass the needle through the two side beads and the top bead from the previous circle. Work all the way up the beading to create the curved shape of the bangle.

9 Join the two ends together on this inner edge by adding side XILION Beads and passing the needle through the first and last XILION Beads on the inside of the bangle. Secure the thread with a half-hitch knot (see page 96) then check that the bracelet is the correct size. It should be a fairly tight fit to go over your hand. If required unpick the last few beads and add more circles of right-angle weave to enlarge the bracelet.

10 Take the needle through the beads to emerge ready to fill the gaps to complete the bangle. Add seed beads and XILION Beads to one side to finish the missing right-angle weave sections then fill in the beads on the other side to complete the bracelet.

**11** Bring the thread out through one of the XILION Beads with a hole running across the width of the bracelet. Pick up three orange pearlized seed beads and then take the needle through the XILION at the other end of the ring in the opposite direction so that the seed beads sit in a diagonal line. Work all the way round the bracelet adding three seed beads on every ring.

**12** Take the thread through to the other side and add three seed beads on every ring on that side too. Make sure the seed beads are going on the opposite diagonal so that you get the attractive chevron effect from the side edge. Sew in the thread end using a half-hitch knot (see page 96) to secure the thread between crystals. Apply a dot of beading glue over the knot and then trim the end.

# *more...*
# BRIGHT *and* BOLD

XILION Beads with their bicone shape work extremely well in right-angle
weave, making an exquisite bead fabric that looks like encrusted barnacles,
but by changing to smoother beads the beaded fabric becomes even
and flat. These variations use tiny cylinder beads and XILION Beads in
different ways to create a selection of gorgeous bright and bold accessories.

**CROCHET AND CUBES ...**
*necklace*

**FLORAL TRESSES ...**
*hair bauble*

**CRYSTAL STACKS ...**
*ring*

# CROCHET and CUBES

Sometimes you just browse around in a bead shop but then other times something immediately catches your eye and you are instantly inspired, and so it was with these fabulous crochet beads. The vibrant colours work well together and when teamed with chunky right-angle weave beaded beads make a fantastic flamboyant necklace. The beaded beads are made from a rectangle of right-angle weave that is joined to make a tube, you then simply fill in the two remaining sides to create the cuboid. For the materials list and instructions, turn to page 112.

# FLORAL *tresses*

Bead weaving motifs, like the flower embellishment on this pretty hair bauble, are worked in a technique similar to right-angle weave. The basic technique has been used to create a crystal tube and if you're wondering how the elastic band gets inside, the fourth row of right-angle weave is actually worked after the part-made tube has been wrapped around the hair band. The flower is made separately and then stitched to the elastic as well as the crystal tube, keeping the metal fastening section hidden inside. For the materials list and instructions, turn to page 122.

## *crystal* STACKS

Right-angle weave worked as a tube using evenly shaped cylinder beads makes
a surprisingly comfortable band for a ring and can be made to fit any size of
finger quite easily. It seems almost impossible but the crystal stacks on this
funky ring are stitched into the ring band and the ends are simply sewn in to
create a neat and professional finish. Unlike the other designs in this chapter
the beads are stitched together using a fine monofilament thread, also known as
illusion cord. This thread is much stiffer and creates a firm ring band that holds
its shape and ensures that the stacks all stand up straight. For the materials list
and instructions, turn to page 117.

# COOL and CHIC

Icy blue and clear crystals work together to create such a frosty effect in these stunning pieces of netted jewellery that they almost look too cold to touch. Clear seed beads with a rainbow or AB finish and white Swarovski Beads with a pearl or Ceylon finish enhance the sub-zero effect.

## OGALALA *lace* NECKLACE

Like many beading techniques, the effect you achieve with Ogalala lace looks different depending on the beads that you use. In this design the netting itself has clear, White and Opal XILION Beads that are almost invisible and a dark core of Pacific Opal and Light Azore XILION Beads running through the middle. Although Ogalala lace looks quite intricate it is a fairly easy technique to work. The crinkly appearance comes with the last row of beads and isn't netting at all, but a simple picot effect. By adding groups of seed beads to make tiny triangles all along the edge you get the attractive crenulated effect and the extra beads also cause the netting to twist and curl spectacularly.

## YOU WILL NEED

- 10g Ceylon translucent white seed beads, size 11
- Bead stringing wire, 60cm (24in) of 19 strands, 0.18mm
- S-lon beading thread in white, size D
- Silver-plated necklace fastening
- 2 silver-plated calottes
- 2 silver-plated crimps, size 1
- 2 silver-plated jump rings
- Crimp pliers
- Basic tool kit (see pages 94–95)

SWAROVSKI ELEMENTS

- XILION Bead 5328 – Light Azore (361) 4mm x 61, Pacific Opal (390) 4mm x 60, Crystal (001) 4mm x 40, White Opal (234) 4mm x 40, White Alabaster (281) 4mm x 40

1 Cut a 60cm (24in) length of bead stringing wire. Beginning with a Light Azore XILION (5328 4mm 361), string alternate Light Azore and Pacific Opal XILION Beads (5328 4mm 390) until there are 61 Swarovski Beads in total. Centre the crystals and attach a small bead stopper spring at each end to secure the crystals temporarily (see page 106).

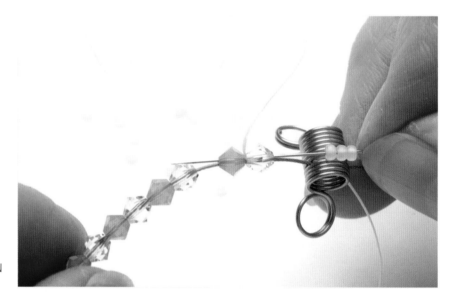

2 Thread a needle with a 1.5m (1½yd) length of thread. Secure the thread in the bead stopper spring leaving a 15cm (6in) tail. Pass the needle through the first XILION, pick up three seed beads and circle through the first XILION again and through the next XILION.

3 Continue down the bead strand, picking up three seed beads and working backstitch through each crystal. Pull the thread taut as you work and then secure the thread in the bead stopper spring at the other end.

4 Attach a third thread in the main strand of beads using one or two half-hitches (see page 96). Pass the needle through the second of the three seed beads over the first XILION Bead. Pick up two seed beads, a XILION Bead (5328 4mm 001), and two more seed beads. Pass the needle through the second of the three seed beads over the next XILION Bead along.

*If you run out of thread, sew in the end using one or two half-hitches (see page 96) and then bring a new thread out at the same bead.*

5 Continue down the bead strand, adding two seed beads, a White Opal XILION Bead (5328 4mm 234) and two seed beads before passing the needle through the next centre seed bead. Next time add a White Alabaster XILION Bead (5328 4mm 281). Work down the strand, repeating the sequence of XILION Beads from Crystal to White Opal and then White Alabaster.

6 Pull the thread taut as you go and add a half-hitch (see page 96) from time to time to prevent the thread loosening. Take the thread through the beads to the main strand again, work a half-hitch and then bring the thread back out through the last XILION Bead added.

7 For this row, pick up three seed beads, a Swarovski XILION Bead (5328 4mm 001) and three seed beads then pass the needle through the next XILION Bead along. Continue adding this seven seed bead sequence between the XILION Beads from the previous row. Change the XILION Bead each time from Crystal to White Opal and then White Alabaster.

8 Secure the thread with a couple of half-hitches (see page 96). Add a new thread if required. Now begin to add a picot edge along the whole length of the bead netting to create the lace effect. Pass the needle through the first of the three seed beads just added in the last row. * Pick up three seed beads and pass the needle through the third seed bead. Pick up three seed beads, miss the XILION Bead and pass the needle through the next seed bead along. Repeat from * until you have worked all the way down the bead strand. Secure the thread end.

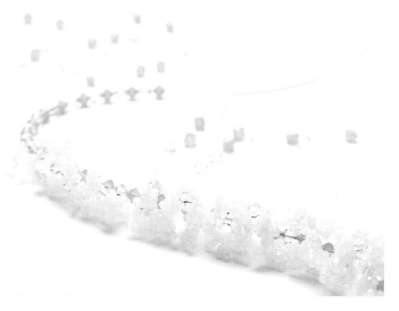

9 Pick up another 30 XILION Beads, keeping the sequence going and alternating between Pacific Opal (5328 4mm 390) and Light Azore (5328 4mm 361) then secure temporarily with a bead stopper spring.

**10** Add a crimp bead to the bead stringing wire with crimping pliers and trim the end close to the end of the crimp. Open a calotte and squeeze closed over the crimp. Push the beads along the beading wire so that they butt up against the calotte. Crimp the wire close to the last bead at the other end. Trim the wire and attach a second calotte (see page 103).

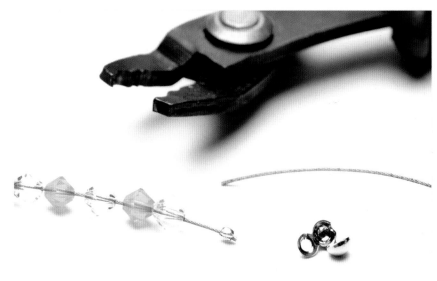

*If you prefer to use a clamshell calotte, feed the bead stringing wire through the hole in the hinge before adding a crimp.*

**11** Use a jump ring or small split ring to attach a necklace fastening to each calotte.

# *more...* COOL *and* CHIC

Netting, one of the most versatile of the bead stitches, can be used to create a tight fabric, a loose mesh or a base for some spectacular fringing. Whether worked flat or three dimensionally, horizontally or vertically, the technique is very similar though the end results are quite spectacularly different.

**KNOTTED CUFF ...**
*bracelet*

**LATTICE CHARM ...**
*key ring*

**ICICLE FRINGE ...**
*earrings*

# knotted CUFF

Tiny beads can make big, bold designs, as shown in this stunning knotted bracelet. Worked in horizontal lace, the design is created with a single strand of thread strung back and forwards between the two end bar fastenings. You could simply work the netting the length required to sit around your wrist for a cuff-style bracelet but the large knot looks amazing and is well worth the extra time it takes to string the beads. In this design the bridge beads are the pearlized pony beads and although the beads in between are added in a random order, the pony beads are spaced accurately to ensure the netting band is flat before knotting. Untied the bracelet is about 30cm (12in) long and will fit a 16–17cm (6½in) wrist measurement. For the materials list and instructions, turn to page 115.

# lattice CHARM

Crystals, perhaps because they are made from glass, are often thought of as transparent but there are opal crystals that are translucent, and alabaster crystals, like those used for this gorgeous bead charm, that are opaque. The facets of the alabaster crystals seem to be enhanced because they aren't transparent and it makes the netted bead look really sharp and funky. Circular netting begins with a circle and a star shape formed by adding equally spaced beads. The netting is then worked across the points of the five-sided star shape in each round (see page 111). Once the bead is completed use a long headpin to create a giant bead dangle and attach a short length of chain and a key ring fastening. For the materials list and instructions, turn to page 122.

# ICICLE *fringe*

Vertical netting is worked with several strands of thread hanging vertically
and so although it uses spacer and bridge beads just like horizontal netting,
it is worked in a slightly different way (see page 110). Because there are
multiple strands, vertical netting lends itself to finishing with a fringe, which
gives these chic earrings a long elegant look. To work vertical netting, you can
secure the thread strands from a row of beads, on the edge of fabric such as
a scarf or from multi-strand fastenings. These sterling silver bar ends with
five rings are actually for making bracelets but I took the fastening off. When
working with lots of different threads you can add a needle on each end but a
single big-eye needle can be quickly transferred between the threads and is a
better option. For the materials list and instructions, turn to page 119.

# DARK *and* DANGEROUS

Black jewellery with its monochrome palette oozes style and elegance. These jewellery designs have all these qualities but each item also incorporates a little Gothic or Punk styling, which adds danger to these dark and delightful pieces. Exquisite colours of the SWAROVSKI ELEMENTS colour range like Indian Sapphire, Dark Indigo and Montana bring subtlety and drama to the designs.

## barbed chain NECKLACE

The large jet-black beads in this necklace are Graphic Beads and are very apt for this design. The necklace looks quite ordinary from a distance but as you get closer the dark and dangerous elements emerge: twists of wire that resemble barbed wire and black safety pins joined together in a haphazard way. The safety pins emanate from the Punk era but are used very cleverly in this design to attach the crystals to the chunky chain. Little dangles made with gorgeous dark shades of crystals and Crystal Pearls add a finishing touch.

## YOU WILL NEED

- Black polyester chain, 1m (1yd)
- 28 black safety pins, 22mm (⅞in)
- 8 gunmetal or black headpins
- Dark purple craft wire, 0.9mm (20swg)
- Basic tool kit (see pages 94–95)

SWAROVSKI ELEMENTS

- Graphic Bead 5520 – Jet (280) 18mm x 5
- XILION Beads 5328 – Jet (280) 4mm x 10, Crystal Vitrail Medium (001 VM) 4mm x 10, Montana (207) 4mm x 10, Dark Indigo (288) 4mm x 10, Indian Sapphire (217) 4mm x 10
- Crystal Pearls 5810 – Powder Rose Pearl (352) 4mm x 6 and Night Blue Pearl (818) 4mm x 6

1 Make each of the Graphic Beads (5520 18mm 280) into a bead link with the 0.9mm (20swg) dark purple wire. Make a loop on the end of a 5cm (2in) piece of wire using round-nose pliers and add a Bead.

2 Bend the wire over at a sharp angle at the other end and trim to 7mm (⅜in). Use the round-nose pliers to form a loop again. Make the other Graphic Beads into bead links in the same way.

3 Cut four 7.5cm (3in) lengths of black polyester chain and one 30cm (12in) length. Open the bead link loops, and attach the long piece of chain between two of the bead links. Attach the shorter lengths to the other side of these links and then join the other bead links and chain together to make the necklace.

4 To make some barbed-wire embellishments, cut twelve 7.5cm (3in) lengths of dark purple wire. Bend one piece into a 'U' shape over the round-nose pliers. Fit over one link of the bead chain and then use flat-nose pliers to bend the wire and pull through the chain link twice.

5 Pull the wire carefully so that the tails are parallel and the wire is wrapped neatly round the chain link. Trim the ends to 7mm (⅜in). Add three pieces of barbed wire spaced down each of the short lengths of chain.

6 Using the headpins, make eight bead/pearl dangles. Pick up two 4mm XILION Beads or a XILION Bead and a Crystal Pearl on a headpin. Bend the headpin over at a sharp angle and trim to 7mm (⅜in). Form a loop with the round-nose pliers (see page 100).

7 Make another seven XILION Bead/ Crystal Pearl dangles. Open the loop using flat-nose pliers and attach one dangle near the top of a short length of chain. Close the loop. Add another dangle to that length of chain and then two to each of the other short lengths of chain, varying the positions of the dangles.

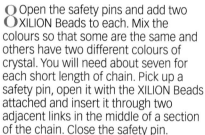

8 Open the safety pins and add two XILION Beads to each. Mix the colours so that some are the same and others have two different colours of crystal. You will need about seven for each short length of chain. Pick up a safety pin, open it with the XILION Beads attached and insert it through two adjacent links in the middle of a section of the chain. Close the safety pin.

9 Pick up another safety pin with two different XILION Beads and insert it through the end of the previous safety pin and a chain link. Continue down the short chain length linking another two safety pins to that group so that the safety pins zigzag down the chain. Attach two more interlinked safety pins at the other end of this short chain length.

**10** Add seven safety pins to each of the short lengths of chain. Make each safety pin sequence slightly different, using various combinations of XILION Beads and arrangements of the safety pins. Look over the necklace and adjust the safety pins or add more bead dangles to create the right effect.

Once the necklace is finished, polish the Graphic Beads with a soft cloth to remove any fingerprints.

# *more...* DARK *and* DANGEROUS

Black or gunmetal chain has none of the delicate prettiness of silver-plated chain and so is the perfect choice to add a dark and dangerous feel to these unusual pieces of jewellery. Although the majority of the crystals are Jet black, subtle dark shades add interest and highlights to the designs.

**SKULL SEDUCTION ...**
*pendant*

**OFF THE CUFF ...**
*bracelet*

**IN THE LOOP ...**
*earrings*

# SKULL *seduction*

Although the majority of crystals used for jewellery are fairly small, you can make a huge impact if you incorporate large stones. This giant pear-shaped Swarovski Pendant would look stunning on its own hanging from a chain but with the addition of a variety of other crystal shapes and an unusual antique silver skull charm it is transformed into a unique piece of jewellery that is just a little edgy. There are so many subtle dark shades in the SWAROVSKI ELEMENTS range, such as Montana, Amethyst and Black Diamond, which add subtle interest to create 'the new black'. For the materials list and instructions, turn to page 112.

# OFF *the* CUFF

Colours are often not what they seem and although it looks black, this chunky bracelet uses lots of dark shades to add intriguing detail to the design. The bracelet is made by plaiting several lengths of chain together with bead ropes to create a cuff-style design. The bracelet can be made with whatever bead stitch you prefer to work in, but tubular twisted herringbone is a little different and very pliable so it is easy to plait. It is much easier to work than flat or even ordinary tubular herringbone as there is no step up – you just keep going round and round (see page 108). Once plaited these fabulous Amethyst Polygons can be incorporated and bead dangles added for extra interest. For the materials list and instructions, turn to page 115.

# IN *the* LOOP

Vitrail Medium is a strange scientific sounding name for a crystal but it is one of the most exotic finishes in the SWAROVSKI ELEMENTS range and is quite unique. A special coating applied over half the crystal adds amazing dark metallic shades creating depth and flashes of colour as the crystal reflects the light. A Vitrail Medium Swarovski Bead can be used with bright colours but comes into its own against black as the rainbow effect is enhanced. String the SWAROVSKI ELEMENTS onto loop earrings and embellish with gunmetal chain and elegant Jet-black polygon Swarovski Beads to make a pair of stunning earrings. For the materials list and instructions, turn to page 119.

# PALE *and* ELEGANT

Simple shapes and subtle shades exemplify pale and elegant style. Clear crystals set off against silver wire and pearls in white and ivory keep the look sparkling and light, while innovative use of exquisite fabrics such as tulle, georgette and silk cord ensure ultimate class and utmost sophistication.

## *tulle* TIARA

Every bride wants to look stunning and this exquisite tiara makes the perfect finishing touch. The pearls and crystals are supported on slender twisted wire stems, which have been graduated to create the basic shape and then the whole tiara is delicately wrapped in bridal tulle for a soft effect. The tulle is secured by wrapping with fine wire with the addition of extra beads nestling among the netting. It is finished with a row of tiny pearls and crystals along the front of the band. It's a beautiful design that gives a hint of a veil for a contemporary bride but will also look fantastic with a traditional veil of matching tulle.

## YOU WILL NEED

- Silver-plated tiara band
- Silver-plated wire, 0.315mm (30swg)
- Ivory bridal tulle, 20 x 40cm (8 x 16in)
- Dressmakers' pins
- Basic tool kit (see pages 94–95)

SWAROVSKI ELEMENTS

- Crystal Pearl 5810 – White (650) 10mm x 2, 8mm x 10, 6mm x 10, 4mm x 40
- Round Bead 5000 – Crystal AB (001 AB) 10mm x 6, 8mm x 5, 6mm x 15
- XILION Bead 5238 – Crystal (001) 4mm x 33

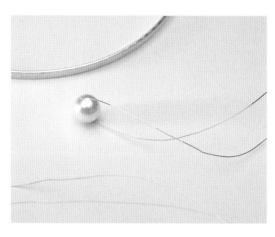

1 Cut a 3–4m (3–4yd) length of 0.315mm (30swg) silver-plated wire and pick up a 10mm Crystal Pearl (5810 10mm 650). Drop the Crystal Pearl down to the middle of the wire and bend so that the wire is going down each side.

Make sure you buy silk or polyester tulle, which is fine lightweight netting with a soft feel rather than the stiffer nylon netting used for petticoats.

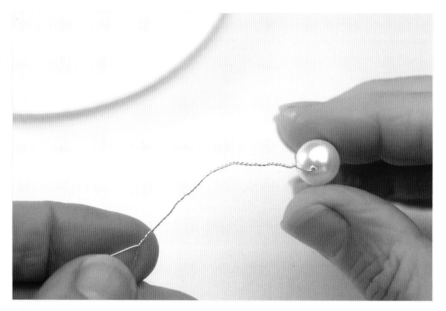

2 Hold both wires about 4–5cm (1½–2in) away from the Crystal Pearl. Twirl the Crystal Pearl around and around between finger and thumb until the wire begins to twist back on itself.

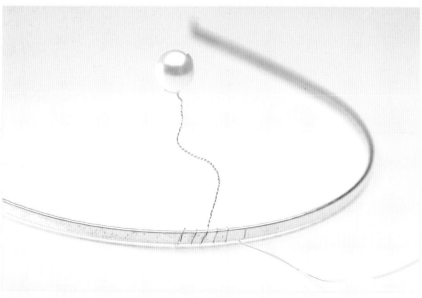

3 Tuck the tiara band between the wire tails and wrap each tail around the tiara band a couple of times to secure the pearl in an upright position.

4 Pick up a 10mm Round Bead AB (5000 10mm 001 AB) on one of the wire tails and drop down to about 4–5cm (1½–2in) away from the tiara band. Fold the wire back down on the other side of the tiara band and hold in place. Twirl the Crystal Bead around until the wire begins to twist back on itself again.

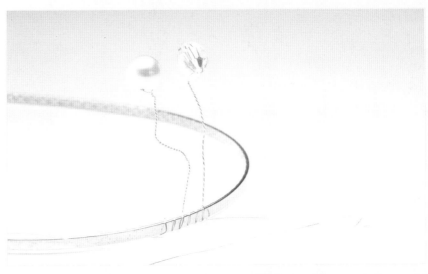

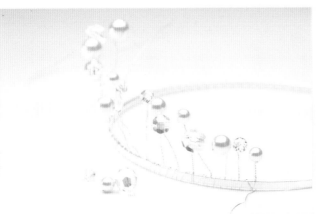

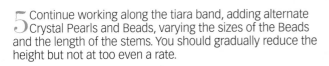

5 Continue working along the tiara band, adding alternate Crystal Pearls and Beads, varying the sizes of the Beads and the length of the stems. You should gradually reduce the height but not at too even a rate.

6 Stop at about 9–10cm (3½–4in) from the centre point around the tiara. Add similar Crystal Pearls and Beads to the other side of the tiara. If you need to join on a new length of wire, twist the ends together, trim and tuck up behind the band.

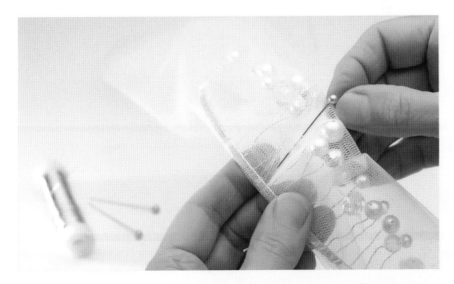

7 Cut a 20 x 40cm (8 x 16in) piece of ivory tulle. Fold the tulle in half lengthways and then wrap around the Beads and tiara band so that the cut edge is facing down on the reverse side and tucked under the folded edge of tulle. Pin in the centre and at several points on each side.

8 Push the folded tulle along the tiara band to gather it slightly. Drop a 6mm Round Bead AB (5000 6mm 001 AB) to the middle of a 2–3m (2–3yd) length of 0.315mm (30swg) wire. Twist the wires to secure the Round Bead and then wrap it around the tulle-covered tiara near the centre so that the Round Bead is sitting at the front.

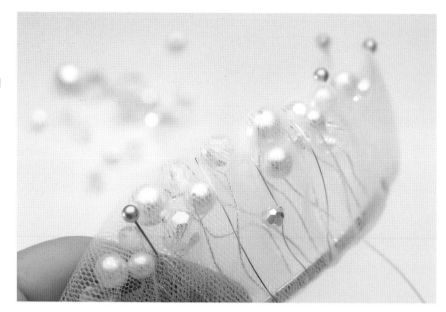

9 Wrap the wire at one side around once and pick up a 6mm Crystal Pearl (5810 6mm 650). Twist the wire to secure the bead on the right side of the tiara again. Wrap the wire around the tulle again and add a XILION Bead (5238 6mm 001). Continue working along the tiara, adding alternate Crystal Pearls and Beads, occasionally adding a 4mm Crystal Pearl (5810 4mm 650) or 4mm XILION Bead (5238 4mm 001) instead.

10 Work along the tiara band gathering and wrapping. As you go, trim away some of the excess tulle so that it is not too heavy towards the end. Wrap the wire around neatly to secure. Complete the other side of the tiara in the same way.

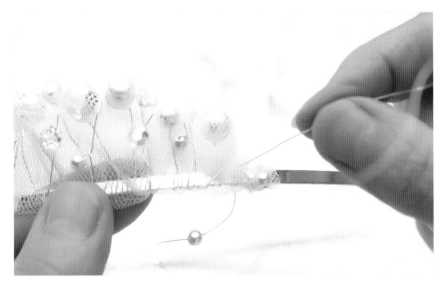

**11** If you have enough wire, work back along or attach a new length of wire at one end of the tiara. With the wire coming from under the tiara band, pick up a 4mm Crystal Pearl (5810 4mm 650) and then 'sew' the wire through the tulle and pull through till the Crystal Pearl is sitting on the front of the tiara band.

**12** Continue along the band alternating 4mm XILION Beads (5238 4mm 001) and 4mm Crystal Pearls (5810 4mm 650) until you reach the other end. Wrap the wire around and 'sew' the end inside the tulle. Check there are no sharp tails of wire sticking down that will scratch the wearer's head.

If you want to keep your tiara as an heirloom piece, use sterling or fine silver wire instead of silver-plated wire.

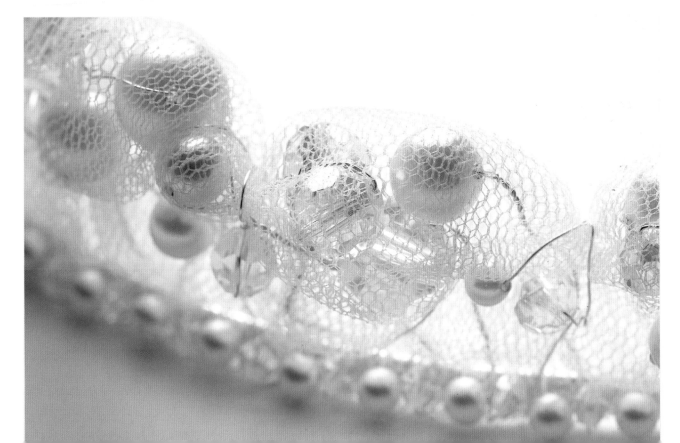

# *more…*
# PALE *and* ELEGANT

All sorts of textiles can be used with beads to soften the effect but you do need to choose the material carefully so that the beads are not overpowered. Like the tulle-wrapped tiara, these projects continue this theme.

**DIVING FOR PEARLS …**
*necklace*

**CRYSTAL CLUSTERS …**
*hair comb*

**PEARL DROPS …**
*earrings*

# DIVING *for* PEARLS

Here is a modern twist on the traditional string of pearls worn by many brides. This design has graduated Crystal Pearls just like the classic pearl necklace, but alternated with crystals for a lighter effect. The beads are strung inside a tubular mesh ribbon, which adds a subtle textured effect, and the Crystal Pearls are spaced with crystal Rondelles to add extra sparkle. For the materials list and instructions, turn to page 113.

# *crystal* CLUSTERS

This exquisite hair comb gets maximum impact from relatively few Swarovski Beads because of the way they are framed by the soft gathers and frayed edges of the pretty silk georgette puffs. The tiny crystals, which set off the white Crystal Pearls beautifully, are suspended almost invisibly on fine twisted wire. You can make the little flower-like puffs with off-cuts from the bridal gown material or even to match bridesmaid's dresses, changing the colour of the pearls and crystals to suit. Reversing the colour scheme completely using dark instead of light colours creates a dramatic effect to add sparkle to you hair for any occasion. For the materials list and instructions, turn to page 123.

# PEARL *drops*

These long elegant earrings will look absolutely divine worn with a stunning
strapless gown as they hang down almost to the shoulders. The simple design
features a hammered solid square ring that reflects the light thrown off by the
gorgeous sparkling SWAROVSKI ELEMENTS. The earrings can be made to
match the necklace on page 55 if you enclose the beads in ivory tubular mesh
ribbon. The ribbon can be gathered around the beads by sewing the tail of the
mesh through the loops at the end of the ribbon. Although fiddly to do, it will
give a very neat finish and secure the mesh tightly round the beads. For the
materials list and instructions, turn to page 120.

# RICH *and* WARM

Rich and warm always brings brown to mind but with the fabulous colours in the warm colour range of SWAROVSKI ELEMENTS, such as Topaz, Padparadscha and Mocca, you just know it is going to be anything but dull. These pieces of jewellery inspired by autumn colours all feature large crystals.

## *cabochon* RING

There is something quite intriguing about a large crystal surrounded by dozens of tiny seed beads because you just want to know how to get the crystal inside. The secret is a beaded bezel, which is like a rim that goes over the edge of the crystal and holds it securely. Although this reduces the size of the crystal, the bezel enhances the depth of the stone and with transparent crystals it is like looking into a deep pool. The actual bezel is worked in circular peyote stitch (see page 107) and then the decorative collar is added afterwards in circular herringbone stitch (see page 107). You can then embellish the ring with other crystals to add texture.

## YOU WILL NEED

- 24 bronze Toho hexagon beads, size 11 (2mm)
- Toho seed beads, size 15 (1mm), 3g each of transparent frosted rainbow medium topaz (A), galvanized pink (B), transparent frosted smoky topaz (C) and silver-lined smoked topaz (D)
- 2g gold Czech charlottes, size 15 (E)
- 2g topaz rose gold lustre Toho seed beads, size 11
- Fireline beading thread in smoke, size D
- Gold-plated ring base and mesh, 10mm
- Basic tool kit (see pages 94–95)

SWAROVSKI ELEMENTS

- Square Fancy Stone 4470 – Smoked Topaz (220) 12mm x 1
- XILION Bead 5328 – Topaz (203) 3mm x 12

*These tiny beads can be difficult to work with if you are long-sighted but a magnifying lamp brings it all into focus.*

1 Pick up 24 hexagon beads on a 2m (2¼yd) length of beading thread and tie in a circle with a reef (square) knot (see page 96) leaving a 25cm (10in) tail. Pass the needle through a few beads to hide the knot (see page 107).

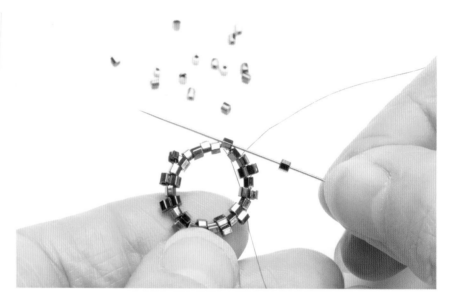

2 Begin peyote stitch: pick up a hexagon bead, miss a bead on the circle and pass through the next bead along. Continue adding hexagon beads one at a time by missing a bead and passing the needle through the next bead along. At the end of the round take the needle through the first bead added to 'step up' ready to begin the next round.

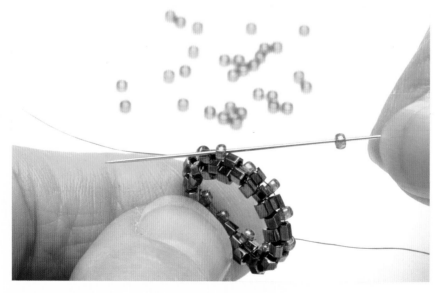

3 Continue in peyote stitch, adding a size 11 rose gold seed bead between each hexagon. Pull the beads tight and step up through the first size 11 bead again then add another round of rose gold seed beads. Finish with a round of size 15A. Pull the beads tight.

4 Secure these beads with a half-hitch knot (see page 96) then take the needle through the beads until you come out at the other side on the top row of hexagon beads. Insert the Square Fancy Stone (4470 12mm 220) right side facing up.

5 Work this side of the bezel in the same way as the underside by repeating step 3, but adding a round of 15E after the 15A. Secure the beads with a half-hitch knot (see page 96) again and then take the needle back through the seed beads to come out in the middle row of hexagon beads.

6 Pick up two size 11 rose gold seed beads and pass the needle through the next hexagon bead. Repeat all the way round, and then pass the needle through the first seed bead again to step up ready to continue in herringbone stitch (see page 107).

7 On the next round work herringbone stitch with size 15B, adding a floating size 15B bead between each stack. Work the next round with size 15C, adding two floating beads between each herringbone stitch.

Tiny size 15 Czech charlottes and seed beads are even smaller than the size 15 Japanese beads and are essential to create a fine edge on the inside of the bezel.

8 On the next round use size 15D, working a herringbone stitch into the two floating beads too all the way round. Work the next round of herringbone stitch with size 15A.

9 For the final round use 15E. Step up through the first stack and pick up three size 15E and pass the needle down through the second bead in the stack to create a picot. Continue all the way round adding three beads to make a pointed end on each stack.

10 Once you have completed the round, secure the thread end with one or two half-hitches (see page 96) and then take the tail through the beads on the right side to come out through the row of hexagon beads visible on the right side. Pick up a 3mm Topaz XILION Bead (5328 3mm 203) and a size 15E. Pass the needle back through the XILION Bead only and then through the next hexagon bead. Continue all the way round adding a XILION Bead and size 15E bead between the hexagons.

**11** Bring the tail out on the reverse side and out through the inner hexagon ring. Position the 10mm mesh from the ring base concave side on the beading and sew in place, securing the thread ends.

**12** Attach the ring base by bending the lugs over the mesh with snipe-nose pliers.

If you prefer. you can use epoxy resin to secure the beading to the ring base instead of sewing.

# *more...*
# RICH *and* WARM

With so many glorious rich, warm colours to choose from in the
SWAROVSKI ELEMENTS range there is no shortage of inspiration
for jewellery with an autumnal feel. Look out for different shapes
such as Round and Oval Sew On Stones or Fancy Stones like the
Cosmic Ring to make more intriguing designs.

**BEZEL FANCY STONES ...**
*brooch*

**AUTUMN ELEMENTS ...**
*necklace*

**COSMIC CORDS ...**
*key ring charm*

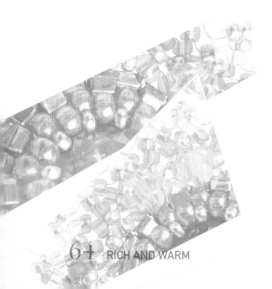

# *bezel* FANCY STONES

The central burgundy Fancy Stone in this fabulous brooch is surrounded by
smaller Fancy Stones and Chatons in different warm but bright colours. Each
stone has a peyote stitch bezel that is created in exactly the same way as the
Fancy Stone in the ring shown on page 59. Although each Fancy Stone is a
different size, you simply start with a different number of beads and then work
the bezel in the same way. The large Oval Fancy Stone begins with 60, the
smaller Oval Fancy Stones and Rivoli Chatons with 28 and the square stone
with 24. You then sew the smaller stones around the large stone to create the
brooch. For the materials list and instructions, turn to page 117.

# AUTUMN *elements*

The rich warm tones of copper, especially if it is antiqued, make a wonderful setting for these large crystals in Copper and Red Magma. which is one of the stunning new colours in the SWAROVSKI ELEMENTS range. It is sometimes difficult to find beads that work with SWAROVSKI ELEMENTS but these Chinese knot beads look fantastic and really enhance the design. The elements for the necklace are either oval or round, which also helps to keep the design unified. Antique copper wire can be tricky to source, but headpins or eyepins are readily available and can be used to create the bead links instead. The wire in these findings is harder than copper wire and so the links will be more secure too. For the materials list and instructions, turn to page 113.

## cosmic CORDS

Rattail is a gorgeous silky cord that can be used to create stunning rope that can be incorporated into a range of jewellery items. Because you create the rope yourself by doubling the rattail. beads and other large elements can be incorporated very securely. To make this key ring charm the rattail has been folded over two large Cosmic Rings and twisted to form a rope. The raw ends are then hidden inside a bell cone end to make the whole design neat and tidy (see page 102). For the materials list and instructions. turn to page 123.

# SEA *and* SHORE

Holidays bring us some of the happiest times in our lives and so jewellery that reminds us of sun-filled days is a delight to wear. These pieces feature fabulous SWAROVSKI ELEMENTS Flat Backs Hotfix in Aquamarine and pale golden colours. Hotfix SWAROVSKI ELEMENTS have a heat-setting glue on the reverse side.

## *seahorse* NECKLACE

Seahorses are much-loved motifs and are often made into charms that are ideal for creating a necklace inspired by the seashore. A charm with one ring at the top can simply be hung from the necklace, or if you find one with a ring at both ends, you can add a crystal dangle at the bottom. The large flat shell beads look stunning with the addition of some Flat Backs Hotfix crystals that create an interesting effect, as the bead string appears to continue right through the middle. Space the round SWAROVSKI ELEMENTS with short lengths of silver-plated chain to create crinkly sections that reflect the intricate pattern on the seahorse charm.

## YOU WILL NEED

- 6 turquoise shell beads, 2.5cm (1in)
- Silver-plated chain, 8 links per 2.5cm (1in), 1m (1yd)
- Sterling silver seahorse charm, 4cm (1½in)
- Softflex beading wire in turquoise, 50cm (20in) of 49 strands, 0.48mm (0.019in)
- 1 silver-plated headpin
- Tubular necklace crimp fastening
- Hotfix tool (see page 104) and tweezers
- 3 silver-plated jump rings, 6mm
- Basic tool kit (see pages 94–95)

SWAROVSKI ELEMENTS

- Round Bead 5000 – Blue Zircon (229) 8mm x 4, 6mm x 18, Aquamarine (202) 10mm x 1,
   8mm x 4, 6mm x 12
- Flat Backs Hotfix XILION Rose 2028 – Blue Zircon (229) SS 12 x 6, Aquamarine (202) SS 12 x
   6, SS 6 x 6, Jonquil (213) SS 16 x 6, Crystal AB (001 AB) SS 5 x 6, Emerald (205) SS 8 x 6

1 String the shell beads temporarily on a piece of Softflex so that you can see where to line up the Flat Backs XILION Rose. Arrange them on the shell bead to check the quantity and size that will fit in a line down the middle between the holes. Tip the Flat Backs Hotfix off onto the work surface.

2 Fit the correct nozzle size for the first Flat Backs Hotfix and heat up the hotfix tool. Pick the crystal up onto the nozzle with a dabbing motion and hold the tool upright for a few seconds until the Flat Backs Hotfix heats up and the glue melts. Position the tip of the tool with the Flat Backs Hotfix inside on the shell bead. Press down for a few seconds and then lift off. If the glue had melted sufficiently the Flat Backs Hotfix will stay on the bead as you lift the tool off.

3 Repeat the process to secure the Flat Backs Hotfix in a row between the holes in the bead. You can add a similar size of Flat Backs Hotfix to the other shell beads as you go to speed up the process. Decorate all of the shell beads with a mix of colours and sizes of Flat Backs Hotfix, placing the larger ones in the middle and smaller ones to fill small gaps at the edge.

Use heatproof gloves to remove the tip of the hotfix tool so that you can change it for another size quickly.

4 Cut 32 five-link lengths of silver-plated chain by snipping through one side of the sixth link along. The cut link should fall away, but if your chain is soldered you will need to cut through both sides of the link (see also page 101).

5 Pick up a 6mm Blue Zircon Round Bead (5000 6mm 229) on a silver-plated headpin. Hold one of the cut pieces of chain and feed the headpin through each link in turn. Pick up a 10mm Aquamarine Round Bead (5000 10mm 202) then another length of chain and another 6mm Blue Zircon Round Bead.

6 Bend the headpin over after the last Swarovski Bead. Trim the tail to 7mm (⅜in) and then form a loop with round-nose pliers. Open the loop and attach to the bottom of the seahorse charm and add a jump ring to the top loop on the seahorse charm.

When adding the chain to the wire, make sure you don't miss any links as these will stick out at one side, spoiling the neat tube shape.

7 Cut a 60cm (24in) length of Softflex beading wire and string on the seahorse charm, dropping it down to the middle. Add a length of chain to each end of the charm by feeding each link one at a time onto the wire (as in step 5), then a 6mm Blue Zircon Round Bead (5000 6mm 229), a length of chain, an 8mm Aquamarine Round Bead (5000 8mm 202), a length of chain and another 6mm Blue Zircon Round Bead.

8 Pick up one of the shell beads on both ends. Repeat the crystal sequence but this time swap the colours so that the 6mm Swarovski Beads are Aquamarine and the 8mm Swarovski Beads are Blue Zircon. Add another shell bead and then repeat the sequence again to add the third shell bead on each end, finishing with a crystal sequence after the last shell beads on each end.

9 Pick up another seven 6mm Beads with chain links in between on each end, remembering to alternate the colours. Hold the necklace around your neck to check the length. Allowing for the necklace fastening, adjust by adding or removing some of the Beads and chain lengths.

10 Feed one end of the beading wire into the necklace fastening and flatten the end with flat-nose pliers to secure the wire. Pull the wire through from the other end of the necklace until the beads are taut against the fastening. Trim the wire leaving 1.5cm (½in). Insert the tail in the other end of the necklace fastening and flatten with pliers to secure.

# *more...*
# SEA *and* SHORE

Swarovski Flat Back Hotfix can be secured to a variety of materials and surfaces, and as there are several methods to activate the heat-sensitive glue, lots of stunning pieces can be created. To complete the designs add one or two fabulous Swarovski Pendants inspired by the sea and shore.

**ROCK SOLID ...**
*bracelet*

**SHIMMERING SHELL ...**
*pendant*

**STARFISH SPARKLES ...**
*earrings*

# ROCK *solid*

Many of the Fancy Stones in the SWAROVSKI
ELEMENTS range come with settings in different
metal finishes. These settings have holes that allow
the beads to be strung together though it can be
difficult to find beads with similar holes. You can
use polymer clay to make beads of all shapes and
sizes but the hardened clay melts if you try to use
a heat tool to add the crystal. As the clay is baked
in the oven to harden, a 'Eureka!' moment made
me realize you could simply position the crystals
on the beads before baking and the heat of the
oven would melt the glue (see page 105). A little
experimentation and this beautiful chunky bracelet
was created. For the materials list and instructions,
turn to page 116.

## *shimmering* SHELL

Swarovski Flat Backs Hotfix have been used to completely cover the surface of
innumerable objects from boxes to mobile phones, often incorporating intricate
designs and interesting patterns. It is tricky creating motifs when you use a
range of different sizes of hotfix crystals, as you need to change the tip on the
heat tool for each size (see page 104) but you can cover objects in a random
design fairly easily. This opulent crystal-encrusted bead is created from a
pressed cotton ball, to which the glue sticks readily, and is then combined with
an iridescent crystal shell to create a striking pendant. Alternatively the bead
could be used create a dangle for a key ring or bag charm. For the materials list
and instructions, turn to page 114.

## STARFISH *sparkles*

Who can resist these delightful Starfish Pendants? They are just the right size for a pair of earrings and look fantastic dangling from some fine silver chain. The earring findings are quite special too – made from sterling silver they have three holes along the bottom edge but one hole has been cleverly covered when they were embellished with a few Swarovski Hotfix Crystals. Swarovski Pendants are also available in a range of sizes and the giant 40mm version would make a stunning matching pendant. For the materials list and instructions, turn to page 120.

# TUTTI FRUTTI

*Tutti frutti* is Italian for 'all fruits' and these pieces of jewellery certainly look good enough to eat. The fabulous SWAROVSKI ELEMENTS in juicy colours are even more mouth-watering when teamed with silver chain and findings, and with such fresh and pretty elements, the designs all have a bright young look.

## *galactic* NECKLACE

Chain is now available in a huge range of styles, sizes and materials and you can mix and match to make really stunning jewellery. If you choose two quite different styles, one with extra large links and another with tiny links, the effect you create shows that two are definitely better than one. Much of the time when making bead links or bead dangles, you can use a simple plain loop (see page 100) but as these large galactic crystals are so precious it is better to use the wrapped loop technique. It can be tricky creating the loops and linking them with the next element at the same time but the secret is to pre-form the loops before you join the bits together (see page 100).

## YOU WILL NEED

- Sterling silver chain, 60cm (24in) with round 4mm links
- Silver-plated chain, 60cm (24in) with oval 2cm links
- Silver-plated wire, 0.6mm (24swg)
- 3 silver-plated jump rings or split rings, 6mm
- Sterling silver trigger clasp
- Basic tool kit (see pages 94–95)

SWAROVSKI ELEMENTS

- Galactic Bead 5556 – Crystal Red Magma (001 REDM) 15 x 27mm x 1
- Galactic Vertical Pendant 6656 – Tanzanite (539) 27mm x 1
- XILION Bead 5328 – Padparadscha (542) 8mm x 1, Indian Pink (289) 8mm x 1, Peridot (214) 8mm x 1, Tanzanite (539) 8mm x 1
- Round Bead 5000 – Peridot (214) 8mm x 1, Aquamarine (202) 8mm x 1, Citrine (249) 8mm x 1, Tanzanite (539) 8mm x 1

1 To create the Galactic Bead Pendant cut a 20cm (8in) length of silver-plated wire and pre-form a loop using round-nose pliers about 5cm (2in) from one end of the wire. Kink the wire 2mm (⅛in) from the loop with snipe-nose pliers to allow for the wrapping.

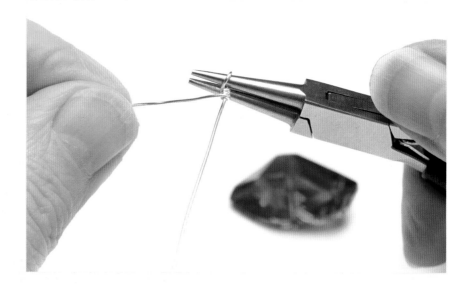

2 Hold the loop in the round-nose pliers and wrap the tail of wire around the main wire two or three times. Trim the tail off using the tips of wire cutters. Add the Red Magma Galactic Bead (5556 15 x 27mm 001 REDM) and put to one side.

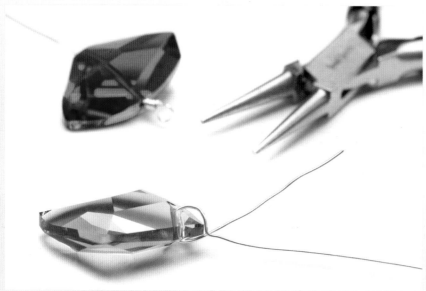

3 Pre-form a large loop as before using round-nose pliers so that it will fit comfortably through the hole in the Galactic Pendant (6656 27mm 539). Insert the wire through the Bead hole. Hold the edge of the loop with snipe-nose pliers, close to where the wires cross, and then wrap the wire two or three times. Trim the tail.

4 Pick up the Round Stone Citrine (5000 8mm 249) on the wire. Bend the wire over about 2mm (⅛in) from the Bead using snipe-nose pliers. This creates the gap for wrapping. Pre-form a small loop with round-nose pliers.

5 Insert the loop you've just formed into the loop of the Galactic Bead made in step 2. Hold the new loop with snipe-nose pliers and then wrap the wire round the gap between the loop and the Round Bead. Wrap the wire around two or three times and trim the tail.

6 Cut the fine chain into nine lengths each with 15 links. Each chain length will be about 4.5cm (1¾in) long. If the chain you are using doesn't have soldered links you can open the links with pliers instead (see also page 101).

Fine chain with open links may not be strong enough to support the weight of these large SWAROVSKI ELEMENTS so look for sterling silver chain with soldered links.

7 Cut a 10cm (4in) length of wire and pre-form a loop about 2.5cm (1in) from the end again. Insert one of the cut lengths of chain into the end link. Wrap the tail around to make the wrapped link as before and trim the tail.

8 Pick up one of the large Round Stones and pre-form a loop at the other side, again remembering to bend the wire with snipe-nose pliers to leave a gap for wrapping the wire (as in steps 4 and 5). Join on a second length of chain and complete the link.

9 Join all the lengths of chain together with the large Beads as wrapped links in between. Alternate between the 8mm XILION Beads and the 8mm Round Stones and make sure no two adjacent Beads are the same colour.

10 Fold the large link chain in half to find the centre front, which is two links side by side rather than one link. Feed the beaded chain through the links from the centre out. One end of the chain goes through one link and the other end goes through the adjacent link. Feed the chain and Beads all the way through to the ends of the large chain links. Secure the two chains together at each end with jump rings or, for extra security, small split rings.

**11** Pre-form a loop at the top of the Galactic Bead Pendant that you prepared earlier. Fit the middle link of the fine chain into the loop. Holding the loop with snipe-nose pliers, wrap the wire around to fill the gap between the loop and the Bead.

**12** Trim the tail using wire cutters. Attach a trigger fastening to the jump ring at one side of the necklace. Attach a short length of the fine chain to the jump ring on the other side to create an extension chain.

Add a decorative dangle to hang down at the back of your neck by making a headpin dangle with another crystal and add it to the end of the chain.

# *more…* TUTTI FRUTTI

It is exciting coming across a new style of bead and these Octagon
Pendants, like mixed fruit sweets, are so delightful. The two holes
make them ideal for pendant-style earrings or as connectors for
a pretty charm bracelet. Alternatively use juicy crystals in an
assortment of shapes to make a quick and easy ring.

**LUSCIOUS LINKS …**
*bracelet*

**FRUITY CLUSTER …**
*ring*

**RUBY DANGLES …**
*earrings*

# *luscious* LINKS

Charm bracelets are probably the most common styles of bracelet, but this delightful design, featuring these fabulous Octagonal Connector Pendants, is in a league of its own. The bracelet is made using two unusual chains with long links, one half the size of the other. If you can't find this particular chain, look for another style that is quite chunky and just a little bit out of the ordinary. Join the elements of the bracelet with jump rings and finish with a pretty toggle fastening. For the materials list and instructions, turn to page 116.

# FRUITY *cluster*

Ring bases, used to make cluster rings, are available in a range of styles with different numbers of loops in various arrangements. This particular ring base has eight rings and there are three bead dangles on each ring. If you choose a different style the resulting ring will look very similar, but you may need to alter the number of bead dangles so that it forms a neat cluster when worn. You can use all the same shape of Swarovski Beads or 'ring the changes' and use several different styles. For the materials list and instructions, turn to page 118.

# RUBY *dangles*

Usually earrings have the weight or focus bead at the top or the bottom, but this unusual design has the eye-catching Octagonal two-hole Pendants bang in the middle. These connector Pendants are ideal for attaching to Bead links and the large holes allow the links to move about creating delightful dangly earrings. Although the Beads in the links appear to be the same size, the top Jonquil Bead is slightly smaller than the bottom Bead and this helps to give the earrings a balanced look. For the materials list and instructions, turn to page 121.

# THE SWAROVSKI ELEMENTS

Crystal is a special material combining transparency and reflections at the same time. Swarovski crystal, precision cut to perfection in a huge variety of shapes, is renowned for its amazing radiance and highest level of clarity that combine to produce a stunning array of spectral colours. Thanks to these unique qualities, SWAROVSKI ELEMENTS Beads reflect colour and light more vibrantly than any other material. The elements used in the making of projects in this book are listed below but this is just a small part of the complete range, which is constantly evolving with new styles, shapes and colours being made available every year.

## Finishes

As well as a huge variety of colours – some classic colours that replicate actual gemstones and other exclusive colours that reflect up-to-date trends – there are diverse finishes or effects that widen the range of SWAROVSKI ELEMENTS considerably. The most well known surface effect is AB or Aurore Boreale, which gives a rainbow effect on clear SWAROVSKI ELEMENTS rather like petrol on water. But there are many other finishes, some on the surface such as Dorado or Golden Shadow and others on the reverse side, like Volcano and Vitrail Medium, that shine through transparent SWAROVSKI ELEMENTS. Foiling is the process of mirror coating the reverse of Fancy Stones and other crystals to achieve an even higher brilliance and sparkle. The highest quality is platinum foiling, but most foiled crystals are coated with aluminium. Transparent foiled SWAROVSKI ELEMENTS have amazing depth, a bit like looking into a pool of water, and transform a piece of jewellery.

*The Swarovski Beads in these earrings (page 57) have an Aurore Boreale (AB) finish, which creates a rainbow effect.*

*The Volcano and Golden Shadow Fancy Stones in this key ring charm (page 67) are surface coated for different finishes.*

*The Fancy Stones and Crystal Buttons in this necklace (page 9) have foiling on the reverse side for brilliant sparkle.*

*Foil-backed Rivoli Chatons, which have a conical shape on the underside, give tremendous depth to this ring (page 59).*

# Styles

There are various different styles of Crystals in the SWAROVSKI ELEMENTS range, from Beads to Pendants and Crystal Buttons.

## Beads

Swarovski Beads are easy to use as they have a hole through the centre, allowing for easy stringing. The holes have a rounded edge at each side to prevent thread wear. There are over 30 different shapes in a range of sizes from 2mm to over 20mm that are available in the latest fashion colours, shapes and cuts. XILION Beads, which have the distinctive bicone shape and are available in more than 50 colours, are the most popular Swarovski Beads followed by the Round Stones, but there are other unusual shapes with fabulous names like Briolette, Polygon and Galactic (used for the Tutti Frutti necklace on page 79) that can inspire you to make your jewellery even more innovative and unique.

## Round Stones

These loose SWAROVSKI ELEMENTS have a round shape with a range of different cuts on the top surface such as Rivoli, which looks like bicycle wheel spokes, and XILION, which is the most brilliant crystal cut on the market. Most of these SWAROVSKI ELEMENTS are pointed on the reverse side like the Chaton, making them easy to use with metal claw Settings or ideal for surrounding with a seed bead bezel like the Bezel Jewel brooch on page 65.

## Fancy Stones

Fancy Stones are similar to Round Stones but are available in numerous shapes and sizes up to 32mm, which are either flat backed or faceted. There is a wide colour range in most shapes and some are available with a foil backing for extra sparkle. Fancy Stones are generally used with a Metal Setting, like the Princess Baguettes used for the Rock Solid bracelet on page 75, or surrounded by a seed bead bezel like the Cabochon Ring on page 59. Ring-shaped SWAROVSKI ELEMENTS, available in a range of sizes and geometric shapes, can be used as connectors or Pendants, such as in the Cosmic Cords key ring on page 67.

## Sew-on Stones

These versatile SWAROVSKI ELEMENTS, which have one or more usually two holes on opposite sides, are designed to be sewn onto textiles or accessories, but they are often used as connector beads particularly in wire and chain jewellery, such as in the Autumn Elements necklace on page 66. They either have a Flat Back or are double-faced with a very thin side profile. The large holes make these Beads from the SWAROVSKI ELEMENTS Assortment ideal for threading with thicker cords and ribbons.

## Pendants

Pendants are beads with one hole at the top that allow movement and add interest to jewellery as they dangle seductively. They have a timeless elegance and are available in a wide range of classical and innovative shapes. These Beads, which can be up to 50mm in length, are amongst the largest in the SWAROVSKI ELEMENTS range and add a touch of luxury to your designs. Available in a range of colours and cuts, they work well with other elements forming a solid backdrop for metal charms and other interesting pieces, such as the Skull Seduction pendant on page 45.

## Flat Backs Hotfix

These loose SWAROVSKI ELEMENTS have a flat reverse side coated with heat-sensitive glue, which is activated at 120–170ºC (250–325ºF) with a special tool (see page 104). They are available in a range of shapes such as navette, square and triangle, although the round XILION Rose is the most popular. Round Flat Backs are available in stone sizes SS 3–SS 40 (1.3–11mm), while other shapes are measured in millimetres, and the colour range is increasing all the time. Also available are Flat Backs Hotfix in a 'Pearl Look'.

## Crystal Pearls

Crystal Pearls are made with a unique crystal core and are covered with a silky smooth pearl coating to create the perfect replica of genuine pearls. They are available in a variety of shapes, sizes and hole diameters to accommodate a wide range of end uses. There is a large range of colours that are matched with specific crystals for a coordinated look. Crystal Pearls are sold individually or loosely threaded on strings.

## Rondelles

Rondelles are shaped metal pieces embellished with Round and Fancy Stones that are used as spacers between Beads or Crystal Pearls, such as in the Diving for Pearls necklace on page 55. They are available in a range of sizes and shapes as well as a range of metal finishes. The SWAROVSKI ELEMENTS on Rondelles are generally clear but can be ordered in other colours.

## Buttons

Crystal Buttons can be used in exactly the same way as standard buttons but are also useful Elements in contemporary jewellery. They are available in a range of shapes, sizes and colours. Some Crystal Buttons have two holes cut through from front to back and others have a shank or holes through the reverse side. Round Crystal Buttons were used in the Flora Necklace on page 9.

# BEADS

Beads come in all shapes and sizes, from tiny seed beads to big, chunky beads and with such variety it can be overwhelming deciding what to buy, especially when you are creating jewellery that includes high-quality crystals from the SWAROVSKI ELEMENTS range. You can narrow down your choice to make the task less daunting by opting for particular techniques, choosing seed beads for bead stitching and larger beads for stringing or wirework, but it is essential that the beads you choose enhance rather than detract from the exquisite crystals.

## Seed beads

Seed beads or rocailles are tiny glass beads often used for bead stitches or netting. They are available in a variety of shapes and finishes creating a huge range of beads to choose from. Most of the top quality seed beads come from Japan or the Czech Republic and these are the most uniform in size. Sizes range from petite (size 15) to pebble (size 3). Some seed beads, such as charlottes and two-cuts, have one or more facets cut on the side to add extra sparkle and interest to a design.

*Regular seed beads can be used for netting techniques (see pages 110–111) because the slight variations in size don't cause a problem, as in the Knotted Cuff bracelet on page 35.*

*Cylinder beads are best suited to bead stitching techniques (see pages 106–109) as the beads butt together neatly, as in the Crystal Stacks ring on page 27.*

*Look out for seed beads in matt finishes that allow the sparkly SWAROVSKI ELEMENTS to come to the fore in a design, such as in the Off the Cuff bracelet on page 46.*

*Tiny size 15 Czech charlottes are indispensable when creating the neat seed bead collars that surround and contain the Fancy Stones in the Bezel Jewel brooch on page 65.*

# Large beads

Walk into any bead shop and it is the large beads that immediately catch your eye, whether they are hanging in strings or arranged loose in trays, the wonderful array is just so inspiring. Large beads are available in an amazing variety of colours and shapes and in a huge range of materials from plastic to semi-precious with metal, wood and fabric to name but a few in between. In reality you can use any large bead you want in a design with SWAROVSKI ELEMENTS but a little trial and error will enable you to choose beads that look fabulous and also enhance rather than detract from the crystals. Although SWAROVSKI ELEMENTS are extremely high quality it isn't necessary to choose expensive beads to complete your jewellery, but a contrasting shape, texture or finish is crucial.

Nothing beats going into a bead shop and actually selecting the beads by hand but if that isn't possible there are hundreds of shops online. When ordering online it is essential to know how to measure beads as they are not generally shown actual size: round beads are measured across their diameter, square beads along one side, and oblong or cylinder beads by length and width. If you are designing a piece of jewellery using thong or cord, consider the diameter of the hole too as this is not always in proportion to the size of the bead, although you can enlarge the hole of some beads with a bead reamer (see page 94). Finally although most bead holes are in the centre and horizontal, you can get beads with off-centre or vertical holes so before buying look closely at photographs to see exactly where the holes are positioned.

*Bone or wood is a good foil for crystals and inexpensive textile beads – such as felt, crochet or Chinese knots – work extremely well too, as in the Crochet and Cubes and Autumn Elements necklaces on pages 25 and 66.*

# TOOLS AND MATERIALS

There are lots of tools and materials that you can use for jewellery making but you will not need everything before you begin. A few basic tools is all that is required to get you started and then you can buy other materials as needed.

## Basic tool kit

### Jewellery tools
You will need round-nose pliers for making loops, flat- or narrow snipe-nose pliers for general holding and manipulating of wire and findings, and wire cutters.

### Beading mat
Inexpensive textured mats are indispensable for beaders. The fine pile stops beads rolling around and lets you pick up directly onto the needle. Once finished it is easy to fold the mat and tip the beads back into their containers.

### Needles
Beading needles have very slender eyes so that they go through seed bead holes. Size 10 is a good general size, and size 13 for fine work. Longer beading needles bend and break readily so keep a good supply. Other useful needles are twisted-eye needles, which have a collapsible eye, and big-eye needles for threading thicker cords and ribbons.

### Bead stopper springs
These are extremely useful little gizmos that can be clamped onto wire or thread to stop beads from falling off or to hold beads taut when stitching with beads.

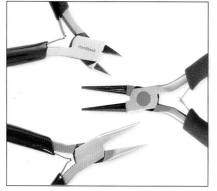

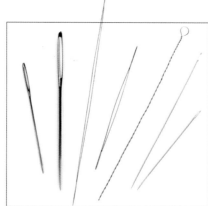

# Other materials

## Specialist tools

Crimping pliers for neat and secure finishing of crimps, a bead reamer for enlarging bead holes, a cup bur for rounding off wire ends and split-ring pliers will all prove useful.

## Thread

Multifilament threads like Nymo, KO and C-lon, which come in a wide range of colours, are ideal for bead stitching (see page 106). Braided threads like Fireline and PowerPro are more suitable for bead stringing and are available in neutral colours. Nylon monofilament threads are strong with a slight stretch, which is useful for working netting over beads (see page 111). Clear elastic thread is ideal for making bracelets without clasps that can be slipped over the wrist.

## Cords, thong and ribbon

Round cords vary in thickness from the slender, slightly stiff waxed cords to the thicker, softly draping silky rattail, which makes a gorgeous twisted rope (see pages 15 and 67). Leather and suede thong is available in round or flat and can be natural or faux. Various ribbons from organza to velvet can be used in jewellery designs.

## Bead stringing wire

Bead stringing wire is a nylon-coated wire made up of a number of strands of stainless steel wire. Brands include Softflex, Beadalon and Acculon Tigertail. Three and seven-strand wires like Tigertail are inexpensive and are a good basic stringing material but wires with 19 or even 49 strands have much more drape and are easier to use for all styles of jewellery.

## Chain

Chain has become widely available in a range of link sizes, styles and metal colours. Some chain links are soldered so that even fine chains are very strong, while other generally less-expensive chains have links that can be opened and closed.

## Findings

These are all the metal bits that make beadwork into jewellery. You can buy most findings in silver- or gold-plated as well as a range of other metal finishes. Pure metal findings are non-allergenic but more expensive. Earring wires, ring bases, clasps, jump rings, bails, headpins and eyepins are some of the items you can use for jewellery.

## Wire

Jewellery wire is generally copper-based with plating for silver and gold or enamelling for a wide range of colours. Wire thickness is measured in millimetres (mm) or standard wire gauge (swg), the larger the swg number the thinner the wire. A good general thickness for jewellery making is 0.6mm (24swg).

## Glues and adhesives

Glues for jewellery making, such as jewellery cement, are designed to stay pliable so that there are no hard knots in beadwork or lumps on bead strings. Choose a glue that dries clear so that it is not visible. Stronger glues, such as epoxy resin, can be used to stick brooch backs in position.

# TECHNIQUES

Many of the techniques used in the designs are clearly shown in the step-by-step instructions for the main project in each chapter but if there is a different technique or variation, it is shown here so that you can complete all the designs as easily as possible.

## Knots

There are several simple knots that are used in jewellery making that will ensure your pieces remain intact and fastenings firmly attached. For extra security, add a drop of jewellery glue on the knots and leave to dry before trimming the tails.

### Reef (square) knot

This is the basic knot for two threads of equal thickness. It is fairly secure but can be loosened by tugging one end. To tie, pass the left thread over the right and tuck under. Then pass the right thread over the left and tuck under the left thread and through the gap in the middle of the knot.

### Overhand knot

Use this knot to tie a bundle of threads together or to tie a knot for a small knot cover (see page 103). To tie, simply cross the tail over the main thread to make a small loop then pass the tail under the thread and back through the loop. You can manoeuvre the knot into position with a tapestry needle.

### Figure-of-eight knot

This knot is an alternative to an overhand knot for knot covers (see page 103). It makes a larger knot that is less likely to pull through the hole in the hinge or side. To tie, cross the tail in front of the main thread and hold between your finger and thumb so that the loop is facing towards you. Take the tail behind the main thread and pass through the loop from the front. Pull both ends to tighten.

### Lark's head knot

Use this knot to attach cords and thongs to rings and pendant beads. Fold the cord in half and take the loop you have made through the ring from the reverse side. Pass the tails through the loop and pull up to tighten. To make a reverse lark's head knot pass the loop through the ring from the front to back and complete the knot by passing the tails through the loop again.

### Half-hitch knot

This knot is generally used to secure threads in bead stitching or when stringing beads with thread. To tie, take the needle behind a thread between beads and pull through leaving a loop. Pass the needle back through the loop and pull up to make the half-hitch. Work a second half-hitch a few beads along for extra security, applying a drop of jewellery glue before trimming the tail.

# Working with wire

Wire-based jewellery is one of the most satisfying crafts to learn as the techniques are easy but produce stunning results in a minimal amount of time.

## Cutting wire

Wire cutters have a flat side and an open side. The flat side cuts a straight edge and the open side cuts a tapered edge. Some high-quality wire cutters cut both ends of the wire straight and fine-tipped cutters give neater results.

1 Cut wire with the flat side of the wire cutters towards the work to get a straight cut on the end. Make sure the jaws are perpendicular to the wire to get a straight rather than an angled cut.

2 When cutting a wire that crosses over another wire, use the very tips of the blades to get as close as possible to the crossover point. Hold the flat side of the wire cutters next to the work.

## Bending wire

Wire doesn't bend on its own. You need to be quite firm to get the wire to bend where you want. Choose flat or snipe-nose pliers and avoid pliers with a serrated surface that will damage the wire.

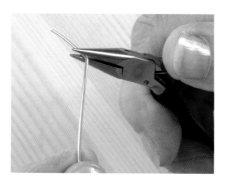

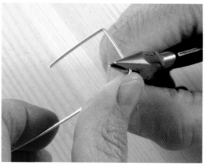

1 Hold the wire firmly with the flat-nose pliers so that the edge of the jaw is exactly where you want the wire to bend. Rotate the pliers to create a particular angle.

2 To make a right angle, hold the tail of the wire and push against the jaws of the pliers with your thumb to exert more pressure.

## Twisting wire

Wire is twisted to create texture and add body so that the wire supports the weight of a bead or so that it holds its shape better. Twisted wire is easier to bend and looks more delicate than an equivalent thicker craft wire.

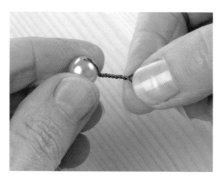

1 Use the bead to give you leverage for twisting the wire. Hold the bead between your finger and thumb and roll it round and round until the wire is evenly twisted along its length.

2 If you are using a thicker wire and find it easier to twist the wires rather than the bead, splay the wires out at right angles so that you can exert a more even pressure to make a neater twist.

# Working with findings

Findings are the metal bits used to finish jewellery, neatening raw ends and making it easy to attach fastenings (see pages 102–103). The type you choose will depend on the materials chosen to make the piece of jewellery.

## Jump rings

Jump rings are round or oval-shaped pieces of wire with a gap for opening or closing. They are generally used to attach findings or to join elements together but can also be used to make decorative chain.

### Making jump rings

1 Choose a rod or knitting needle of the required diameter. Hold the end of the wire at one end and wrap the wire tightly around the rod. Count the number of turns and add a few more turns to allow for trimming.

2 Slide the closely wound spring off the rod. Pull the spring open slightly by hand or with two pairs of pliers. Use wire cutters to trim one end of the wire straight with the flat side away from the tail.

3 Line up the pliers with the first cut so the flat side of the pliers is away from the cut end. Turn the pliers and trim the new end each time with the flat side of the pliers before cutting the next jump ring.

### Opening and closing

1 Hold the jump ring with two pliers, ideally two pairs of flat-nose or use round-nose with a pair of flat-nose pliers. To open the ring, bring one pair of pliers towards you.

2 Pick up another jump ring, chain or finding on the open jump ring. Reverse the action to close.

3 To tension the jump rings so that they stay closed, push the ends slightly so that they overlap on one side and then the other. Pull back and the ends will then spring together.

# Eyepins and headpins

An eyepin is a piece of straight wire with a loop at one end. They are usually used to connect beads or jewellery components, such as simple earrings or bead charms. A headpin has a flat end that looks a bit like a giant dressmaker's pin. They are used to make bead charms that dangle from chain, cord or from an eyepin to create movement in jewellery designs. Shop-bought eyepins and headpins can be made from either soft or hard wire.

## Making an eyepin

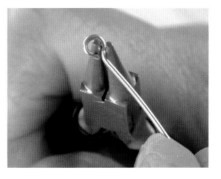

1 Cut the wire straight at the end with wire cutters (see page 97). Hold the wire about 6mm (¼in) from the end of the round-nose pliers so that the tip of the wire is level with the jaws.

2 Bend the wire around the pliers with your thumb, or by turning the pliers, until the cut end touches the main wire.

3 Reposition the round-nose pliers, as shown. Bend the loop back against the jaws until it is central above the straight wire.

## Making a bead link

This is an easy technique for beginners but you can also use the plain loop technique for headpins shown on page 100.

1 Make an eyepin loop on the end of the wire. Pick up the beads you require. Hold the wire in the jaws of the round-nose pliers. Wind the wire around the pliers to make a loop.

2 Cut the wire where it crosses, using the very tip of the wire cutters. Hold the ring with round or snipe-nose pliers and bend back to straighten.

3 To join the links together or to a headpin charm, open one of the loops by pushing the cut end back, attach the next section and then close by reversing the action. Attach an earring wire in the same way.

## Plain loop

This is an alternative, more professional technique for making a loop on headpins, eyepins or wire. If the bottom bead slides over the headpin end, add a smaller bead, such as a seed bead first.

1 Trim the headpin to 7mm–1cm (⅜–½in) above the top bead. The distance will depend on the thickness of the wire and the size of loop required. Make a right-angle bend close to the bead using snipe-nose pliers.

2 Hold the tip of the wire with round-nose pliers and rotate the pliers to bend the wire partway around the tip. Reposition the pliers and continue rotating until the tip touches the main wire. Check the position of the loop and adjust until it is central.

## Wrapped loop

The wrapped loop is stronger and more secure than a plain loop. It is ideal for beads with slightly larger holes or for more precious beads like Swarovski crystals that you don't want to lose. Use longer headpins to allow for wrapping. If you find it difficult to wrap by hand, use flat-nose pliers for more grip.

1 You will need at least 3cm (1¼in) of wire above the last bead. Using snipe-nose pliers, hold the wire above the bead leaving a small gap and bend at a right angle.

2 Hold the wire close to the bend with round-nose pliers and wrap the tail all the way round to form a loop.

3 Hold the tail firmly with flat-nose pliers and wind the tail around the stem covering the gap between the loop and the bead. Trim the tail.

## Wrapped loop chain

As wrapped loops are closed loops, when making a chain or joining a bead charm and bead link you need to pre-form the next loop then add to the previous ready-made wrapped loop before completing the next wrapped loop.

1 To make the first wrapped loop, use round-nose pliers to create a loop at least 3cm (1¼in) from the end of a piece of wire. Hold the loop in snipe-nose pliers and wind the wire around. Trim the tail.

2 Add the beads required and make a wrapped loop after the beads as described for the wrapped loop above. Pre-form the loop for the next bead link on another piece of wire. Insert the bead link into the loop.

3 Hold the loop you are making with snipe-nose pliers and then wind the tail around the main wire to complete the wrapping. Trim the tail. Repeat steps 1–3 to continue the chain.

# Working with chain

Chain is available in different metals and finishes in a huge variety of styles that range from fine to big and chunky. Some links, especially precious metal chains, are soldered and others have open links.

## Cutting chain

Measure the length of chain required and then cut through the next link on one side. If the chain is thick or made with soldered links cut through both sides so that the link falls away. On chain with large links you can open a link to separate the lengths.

## Joining chain to fastenings

Open a jump ring with two sets of pliers, loop through the last link in the chain, add the fastening and then close the jump ring with a reverse action (see page 98). If the chain has links that aren't soldered you can open the last link instead to add the fastening.

## Threading chain

If you thread elastic, thread or wire through the links in chain it will scrunch up and become very close packed and textured. Thread a whole chain with elastic to make a bracelet or thread short lengths onto wire to make bead spacers, as in the Seahorse Necklace on page 69.

## Antiquing chain and findings

Chain and jewellery components can be aged to give them an antique look in minutes. You can buy patinas for a range of metals but the most common used in jewellery making is liver of sulphur for silver or silver-plated wire. You can antique the jewellery with most beads, including Swarovski crystals, attached although bone, ivory and polymer clay are not suitable.

1 Working in a well-ventilated area, drop a chunk or a few drops of liquid liver of sulphate into a bowl of hot (not boiling) water and stir to dissolve. Use pliers to lower the jewellery until it is submerged. Leave for a short while until the desired dark shade is achieved, then rinse in lukewarm water and pat dry.

2 You can leave the findings black, a technique used to create the gunmetal multi-strand fastenings on the Off the Cuff bracelet on page 46, or clean off most of the blackened surface with a stiff wire brush for an antique look, finishing with fine 0000 wire wool. Polish with a soft cloth to finish.

# Adding fastenings

There are lots of ways to add fastenings, depending on the type of stringing material, the style of fastening and the actual design of the jewellery. Look at the following examples, then choose the method that best suits the piece you are finishing.

## Using cord ends

Thicker threads and cords can be finished simply using one of the many crimp ends available, which are sold in a range of metallic colours.

**Spring crimps** Use flat-nose pliers to squeeze the last ring of the spring into the thong, cord or ribbon, so that it is held securely.

**Leather thong ends** Use flat-nose pliers to flatten one side against the thong. Repeat with the other side so that it is held firmly.

**Crimp fastenings** Some fastenings come with an inbuilt crimp. You simply insert the cord and squeeze the crimp ring to secure. Look out for tubular crimp fastenings and cord ends. Feed the cord or wire into the tubular end and squeeze flat with pliers.

## Using cone ends

Cone ends are used to secure bulky threads, cords or ribbon. Choose a size that fits closely around the material for best results.

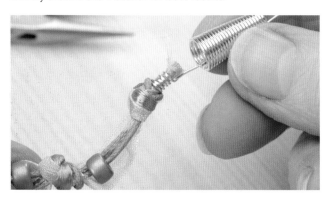

1 Secure the cords, thread or ribbon by wrapping with wire and then feed the tail through the cone.

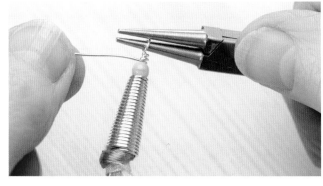

2 Add a small bead if necessary to reduce the hole size on the cone end before finishing with a wrapped or plain loop (see page 100).

3 Alternatively for bell cone ends with a loop attached, secure the cords or ribbon with fine wire and trim neatly. Apply jewellery glue over the end and insert into the cone end. Hold for a few minutes until dry.

## Using a crimp

This technique is ideal for bead stringing wire that can't be knotted but can also be used for bead string or elastic thread.

1 Pick up a crimp bead, a jump ring or fastening and take the wire back through the crimp bead. Secure the crimp with pliers. Add beads over both the tail and the main wire.

2 At the other end pick up a crimp and the jump ring or fastening. Feed the wire back through the crimp and several beads. Secure the crimp with pliers and trim the wire end.

## Using a knot cover

This little finding, sometimes known as a calotte or clamshell, is a neat way to finish thread ends securely. A calotte has a hole in the side of the cover and the clamshell has a hole in the hinge, which is generally more secure.

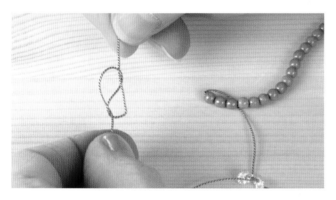

1 Feed the thread through the hole in the hinge and tie an overhand or figure-of-eight knot (see page 96). Push the beads down so that the knot is inside the clamshell. At the other end you can guide the knot into the clamshell with a tapestry needle.

2 Trim the tail and apply a drop of jewellery glue to the knot. Squeeze the sides of the clamshell together with flat-nose pliers to hide the knot. Attach the fastening of your choice.

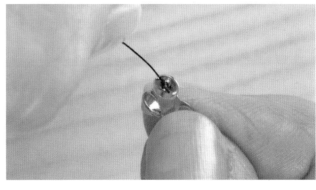

3 If the calotte has a hole in the side, simply attach a crimp bead or tie a figure-of-eight knot at the end of the bead string then trim and apply a drop of glue. Tuck the knot or crimp inside the calotte so that the thread is in the groove and close with flat-nose pliers.

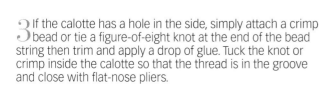

# Special techniques for SWAROVSKI ELEMENTS

SWAROVSKI ELEMENTS are available in a wide range of shapes, from Beads and Pendants to Hotfix Crystals and Fancy Stones. To use some of the more special shapes, follow the step-by-step instructions below.

## Setting a Fancy Stone

Fancy Stones are crystals without holes. They can be flat backed or have a shaped back. Most Fancy Stones are fitted into a specially designed setting ready for use. The settings are available with a range of hole positions to allow a variety of end uses.

1 Insert the stone into the appropriate setting and hold so that it is level.

2 Bend the lugs over one at a time using the flat side of pliers or another suitable tool.

## Flat Backs Hotfix

Flat Backs Hotfix are flat-backed SWAROVSKI ELEMENTS with glue on the back that is activated with heat. Small round Hotfix Beads can be secured with a special heat tool and larger Hotifx Beads can be attached with a domestic iron. Flat Backs Hotfix can also be secured by baking in an oven (see polymer clay opposite).

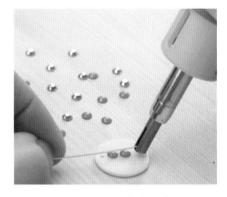

1 Insert the correct tip into the heat tool and plug it in to heat up. Pick up the Flat Backs Hotfix Bead in the tool and hold upright for a few moments to allow the glue to melt.

2 Turn the tool over and carefully place the tip in position. Lift the tool off and the Bead will remain attached to the material. Repeat to stick another Bead of the same size or use safety gloves to change the tip for another size.

3 When applying Hotfix Beads to a smooth shiny material like metal you may need to ease the Bead out with a needle. Insert the needle through the slots in the tip once the glue is melted.

*Make sure the Bead is hot and the glue melted when applying to the shell beads on the Seahorse Necklace. Full instructions are on page 70–73.*

# Working with polymer clay

Polymer clay, which is set by baking in an oven, is a useful material to make beads that can be incorporated into designs featuring exciting SWAROVSKI ELEMENTS such as Fancy Stones in Settings.

1 Knead the clay until it is warmed and softened. Wipe a ceramic tile or smooth work surface with kitchen towel dabbed in vegetable oil. Flatten the ball of clay.

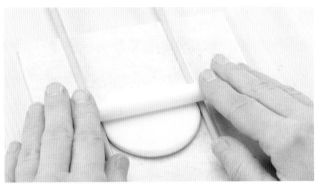

2 Lay knitting needles or skewers the depth you want the beads to be on either side of the clay and roll out with a small rolling pin until the pin is rolling on the knitting needles.

3 Cut the beads with a sharp kitchen knife or cut out shapes with pastry cutters. Use a fine headpin to make the holes and then enlarge the holes with a thicker headpin or wire.

4 You can add Flat Backs Hotfix SWAROVSKI ELEMENTS to the unbaked polymer clay. The crystals will stick temporarily to the surface. Place the tile with beads in the oven or transfer the beads to baking parchment on a baking tray. Bake the clay according to the manufacturer's instructions or for 20 minutes at 120°C (250°F / Gas Mark ½).

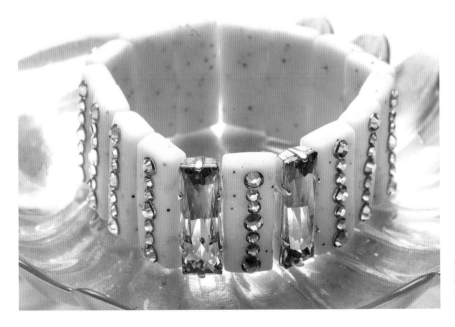

*The Rock Solid bracelet on page 75 was created using this ingenious technique. Full instructions for making it can be found on page 116.*

# Bead stitching

Bead stitching encompasses all sorts of techniques that are used to sew small beads, usually seed beads, together as a bead fabric, rope or tube. There are many different stitches, which create a huge range of different effects but only the specific stitches used in this book are shown here.

## Getting started

You only require a needle and thread for bead stitching but depending on the size of the bead holes, you may need a specific type and size of needle. Beading needles, either short or long, have thin long eyes that go through bead holes easily. Choose a size 10 needle and size D thread for most seed beads but if you are working with tiny charlottes (see page 92), you will need a size 13 needle and size B thread.

Begin with as long a thread as you can manage to save making joins, but if you prefer to work with shorter lengths, or you run out, sew in thread ends and join another length using half-hitches (see page 96) to make the thread secure.

## Threads

Until recently there were only one or two threads available for bead stitching, but now there is a vast range. Look for a thread that is thin and pliable enough to go through tiny bead holes. Multifilament threads like Nymo, C-lon and S-lon are most people's first choice as they are available in such a wide range of colours but many bead stitchers use braided threads such as Fireline and PowerPro instead. These extra-strong threads are only available in neutral colours but are less likely to stretch and are ideal for closely stitched bead fabric.

Ask in your local bead shop to find out about other threads, such as KO, which has a round cross section and is easy to thread. Although monofilament threads are generally too stiff for most bead stitching, you will need a thread with stretch (so that it is less likely to snap) when covering three-dimensional objects in netting (see Lattice Charm, page 36).

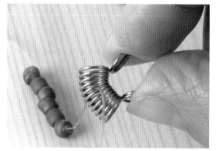

## Conditioning thread

Opinions are divided on the use of conditioners such as Thread Heaven or microcrystalline wax when bead stitching. They are designed to coat the thread to prevent wear and also to prevent knotting and tangling. Conditioned thread tends to keep the beadwork tighter as the thread doesn't slip back through the beads as easily.

Run the thread over the top of the conditioner and then pull through between two fingers to distribute the conditioner and to create static electricity that prevents the thread tangling.

## Bead stoppers

When working some jewellery designs and some bead stitches it is essential to stop the beads falling off the end of the thread or bead stringing wire. Bead stopper springs are a great little tool for this job or use a stop bead instead.

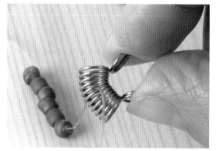

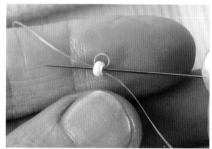

**Bead stopper spring** To use a bead stopper spring, squeeze the levers on the spring and slot the thread between the coils. Move the spring up and down the thread as required.

**Stop bead** To add a stop bead, pick up a bead on the thread and hold about 10cm (4in) from the end. Take the needle back through the bead two or three times to secure.

# Circular peyote stitch

This versatile stitch creates a flat bead fabric that bends horizontally making it ideal for creating bezels around fancy stones and other large flat crystals. There is no decreasing but using progressively smaller beads allows the beadwork to curve in to enclose the stone and grip it securely. The first two rows of beads are strung to begin.

1 String an even number of beads to surround the fancy stone, tie in a circle and pass the needle through a few beads to hide the knot, leaving a long tail. These beads form the first two rows of peyote stitch.

2 Pick up a bead on the needle, miss a bead on the circle and pass the needle through the next bead along. Continue adding beads one at a time by missing a bead and passing the needle through the next bead along.

3 At the end of the round take the needle through the first bead added again to 'step up' ready to begin the next round. The beadwork will now have the distinctive zigzag edge of peyote stitch with 'up' and 'down' beads.

4 Continue adding beads between the 'up' beads remembering to step up through the first bead added in each subsequent round. For a neater effect reduce the size of beads in each round.

5 When you have added sufficient rounds to form a collar, add a final round with tiny beads to make a smooth thin edge on the collar. Take the thread through to the beginning row again.

6 Insert the Fancy Stone face down and repeat the peyote stitch from step 2 to create a second beaded collar that that holds the stone securely.

# Circular herringbone stitch

Herringbone stitch is one of the most distinctive bead stitches because of the 'V'-shaped pattern created by adding two beads at a time. Circular herringbone is easier to learn than flat herringbone, as there are no tricky starting rows. You do however need to add single, then pairs of floating beads in adjacent rounds to increase the number of beads and keep the circle flat.

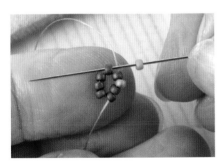

1 Begin with a ring of beads, say seven beads, on a long thread tied in a circle with a reef (square) knot (see page 96). Pass the needle through a few beads to bury the knot. Pick up a single bead between each bead in the base circle.

2 Step up to the next round by going through the last (brown) bead from the previous round and the first (pink) bead added in this round.

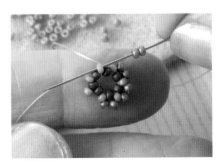

3 Pick up two (khaki) beads between each of the beads you added in the last round. These pairs of beads will form the base of the herringbone stitches. *(Continues overleaf)*

4 Step up again, this time going through one pink and one khaki bead, added in the previous round. Work a round of herringbone into each pair of beads.

5 On the next round add a single floating bead between each herringbone stitch, then two floating beads in the next round. In the next round work herringbone stitch into each herringbone stack as well as each pair of beads added in the next round.

6 Repeat the process adding a single, then pairs of floating beads to increase quickly and keep the beadwork flat.

## Tubular twisted herringbone stitch

This variation of tubular herringbone stitch is created by a simple alteration in the way the thread is routed through the beads causing the bead stack to tilt to one side and then to spiral round as you add further beads. You can begin with any even number of beads.

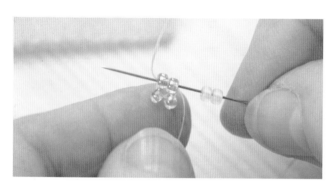

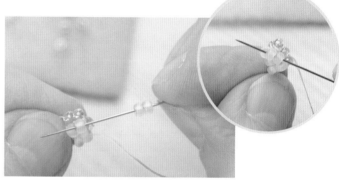

1 To create a two-drop ladder stitch tube base, tie four gloss beads in a circle, * pick up two matt beads and circle through the last two beads. Repeat from * then join the ends together by circling through the end beads. Make sure the thread comes out at the top of the first matt bead ready to work two rounds of plain tubular herringbone stitch.

2 * Pick up two matt beads and pass the needle through the next matt bead along and then back up through the next gloss bead. Pick up two gloss beads and pass the needle through the next gloss bead. As shown in the inset image, step up through two matt beads to complete the round. Repeat from * once more.

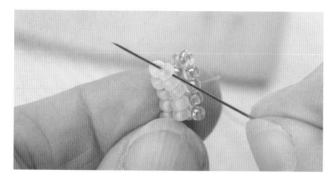

3 To create the twist, on the next round rather than stepping up through two matt beads, take the needle through the top bead only. Pick up two matt beads then take the needle back down through the next two beads.

4 * From now on bring the needle up through the top bead on the next stack and pick up two beads then go back down through the next two beads. Repeat from * and as you are spiralling there is no step up. Simply repeat the 'two down one up' until the rope is the length required.

# Right-angle weave

Right-angle weave is one of the few stitches that are worked in a similar way to make a flat piece or a tube. The basic stitch has four beads in each circle but you can increase the number of beads to make a more intricate design.

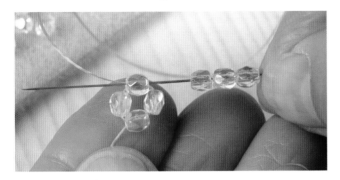

1 Pick up four beads and tie in a circle with a reef (square) knot (see page 96), leaving a long tail. Pass the needle through three beads so that the thread emerges at the opposite side to the tail. Pick up three beads and circle the needle back through the top bead, then through the next two beads in a clockwise direction to the top bead again.

2 Pick up three more beads. Circle the needle through the beads in an anticlockwise direction to come out at the top bead again. Continue adding three beads at a time, alternating the direction you circle through and making sure you come out at the top bead each time.

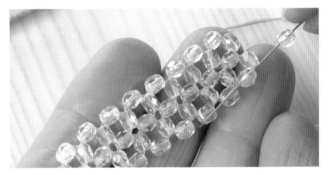

3 To make a wider band, take the needle through the beads to a side bead. Pick up three beads and pass the needle through the side bead again, then circle round until the thread comes out through the bottom bead. From then on, use the beads already on the panel, adding only two beads each time to complete each circle.

4 To form a three-sided tube, bring the needle out again at a side bead. Pick up one bead, pass the needle through the side bead at the other edge and then pick up another bead. Circle through the beads again to come out at the bottom bead. Continue adding one bead at a time to the bottom of the tube. To form a four-sided tube, work a third column of right-angle weave before you join the edges together.

## Adding extra beads

Right-angle weave can be worked with more than four beads. This example keeps the square format with four large beads and four small beads in each unit. You must remember to pick up single small beads as required to complete the pattern.

## Bead weaving

Circular bead weaving designs based on right-angle weave are often shown as a diagram rather than step-by-step instructions. The diagrams show the direction of the thread through the beads, and usually show the starting point and outlines the order that each section is worked. The flower motif from the Floral Tresses hair bauble on page 26 uses a diagram, which is given on page 126.

# Vertical netting

As the name suggests this netting is usually worked with multiple threads vertically, with fringing at the bottom, like the Icicle Fringe earrings on page 37, but the technique can also be used to create cuff style bracelets with a single thread (see Knotted Cuff, page 35). The beading has shared beads spaced out evenly where the netting strands come together, and bridge beads in between.

## Single thread

Working vertical weaving with a single thread between two end bars is one of the easiest netting techniques as there is no shaping required.

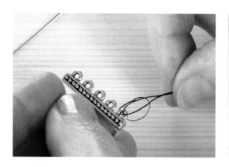

1 Thread the cut ends of a very long double thread on to the needle. Take the needle through the first ring on your end bar and back through the loop to begin.

2 Pick up the required number of bridge beads (in this case 11) and a shared bead. Repeat to get the length required, making sure there is an even number of shared beads ending with the bridge bead sequence.

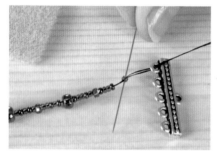

3 Go through the end ring on the other end bar and take the needle back through the last bead.

4 Pick up 10 more seed beads to complete the bridge sequence and a shared bead, then 11 seed beads. Miss a shared bead on the last strand and take the needle through the next shared bead. Repeat to the end.

5 Repeat steps 3 and 4, going back and forwards until all the rings on the end bar are filled. Go back through a few beads, tie a half-hitch knot (see page 96), repeat to make the threads really secure and trim the end.

## Multiple threads

This version of vertical netting is worked with pairs of threads attached to the edge of a scarf or can be worked on a multi-strand end bar to make earrings, as in Icicle Fringe, page 37. The fringe beads can be added to pairs of threads as shown here, or on single threads to give a fuller effect.

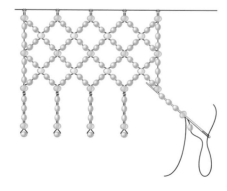

Fold long threads in half and attach one thread to each ring or the edge of fabric using a lark's head knot (see page 96). Begin at one side, picking up all the beads for the sequence on the first strand. For the second strand, pick up beads in sequence, remembering to omit every second shared bead and take the needle through the appropriate shared bead on the first strand. Once the netting is complete with beads added for the fringing, add a pivot bead to each fringe strand, go back through some of the beads and secure the thread with two half-hitches (see page 96).

# Circular netting

Netting can be worked in the round to cover 3D objects like baubles and large beads. The bead sequence can be varied but this shows the basic technique. The shared beads are always single but the bridge beads increase and decrease in number to fit the shape of the bead.

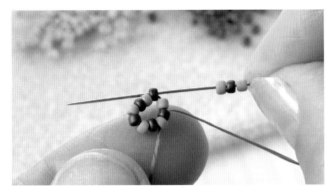

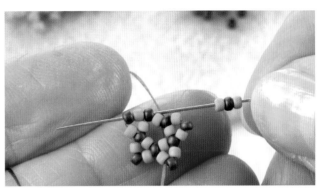

1 On a long length of thread, pick up 10 seed beads in alternating colours, pass the needle through the beads again and tie in a circle with a reef (square) knot (see page 96). Pass the needle through a few beads and out after a shared (dark) bead. Pick up a bridge (light) bead, a shared bead and a bridge bead. Take the needle through the next shared bead.

2 Repeat all the way round. To step up, take the needle through one half of the first loop again coming out after the shared bead ready to begin the next round.

3 Pick up two bridge beads, a shared bead and two bridge beads. Pass the needle through the shared bead in the next loop. Repeat all the way round, stepping up through the first loop in the last round.

4 Continue adding two extra bridge beads on each loop until you reach the mid point of the large bead and then decrease the beads in the reverse sequence to cover it completely. Thread a ring of beads to match the other end and sew in the ends with half-hitches (see page 96).

*The Lattice Charm key ring on page 36 was created using the circular netting technique. Full instructions for making it can be found on page 122.*

# *more...* PROJECT INSTRUCTIONS
## Necklaces

### CROCHET AND CUBES (page 25)

#### YOU WILL NEED
- Cylinder beads, size 11, 5g each of opaque orange and opaque light siam
- Crochet beads, 22mm, orange x 2, pink x 2 and fuchsia x 2
- Deep pink and orange waxed cotton, 2mm, 45cm (18in) of each
- Silver-plated cord end necklace fastening, 3mm
- Jewellery glue
- Basic tool kit (see pages 94–95)

SWAROVSKI ELEMENTS
- XILION Bead 5328 – Fuchsia (212) 4mm x 95, Rose (209) 4mm x 140, Light Peach (362) 4mm x 30

**1** To make the cube bead, work in right-angle weave (see page 109) picking up colours in a random order using more of the Rose XILION Beads (5328 4mm 209) than Fuchsia (5328 4mm 212) and just the occasional Light Peach (5328 4mm 362) to add interest. **2** Pick up a cylinder bead and a XILION Bead four times. Tie in a circle, leaving a 15cm (6in) tail. **3** Work a chain of seven circles in right-angle weave following the steps in the bracelet project on page 20 but using 4mm XILION Beads and cylinder beads. Then work three columns to make a panel three circles wide and seven circles long with the thread coming out at the top XILION Bead at one end. Bring the two short ends together. **4** To join the folded panel into a tube, pick up a cylinder bead, a XILION Bead and a cylinder bead and pass through the XILION Bead on the other side. Continue along adding a XILION Bead and cylinder beads each time to continue the pattern. **5** Fold the tube to make the bead shape with nine squares on each side. Add XILION Beads and cylinder beads to complete the side panels in right-angle weave. Sew in the thread ends securely. Make three more square beads. **6** Work three circles of right-angle weave and join in a ring. Make a second ring the same. **7** String the beads as shown in the picture on page 25 onto orange and pink waxed cotton. Trim the cord ends at an angle, apply glue to the ends and inside the cord end fastening (see page 102). Tuck the ends in and leave to dry.

> When finishing the last two sides you will circle round sometimes only adding in cylinder beads to complete the right-angle weave pattern.

### SKULL SEDUCTION (page 45)

#### YOU WILL NEED
- Silver-plated skull charm, 20 x 12mm
- Black thin trace chain, 11 links per 2.5cm (1in), 50cm (20in)
- Silver-plated chain, 1.5cm (⅝in)
- 8 black headpins
- 3 black jump rings, 6mm
- Basic tool kit (see pages 94–95)

SWAROVSKI ELEMENTS
- Pear-shaped Pendant 6106 – Jet (280) 38mm x 1
- Round Bead 5000 – Black Diamond (215) 10mm x 1, Montana (207) 10mm x 1
- XILION Bead 5328 – Montana (207) 4mm x 2
- Polygon Bead 5205 – Amethyst (204) 15 x 6mm x 2
- Pendant Drop Bead 5310 – Jet (280) 5.5mm x 2

**1** Cut a 2.5cm (1in) length of the black chain and feed through the Jet pear-shaped pendant (6106 38mm 280). Join the ends with a jump ring (see page 98). **2** Make all the beads into headpin dangles with a plain loop at the top (see page 100). **3** Cut a 5cm (2in) length of black chain and attach the Black Diamond 10mm Round Bead (5000 10mm 215) to the bottom. Attach the 5.5mm drop (5310 5.5mm 280) a few links up, then the 4mm Montana XILION Bead (5328 4mm 207) and then a Polygon Bead (5205 15 x 6mm 204). **4** Attach the short length of silver-plated chain to the skull charm and add a 4mm XILION Bead dangle to the first link of chain. **5** Open the jump ring on the Jet pendant carefully and thread on the long chain dangle, the polygon headpin dangle, the skull charm

then the last round headpin dangles and finally the last 5.5mm drop. Close the jump ring (see page 98). **6** Feed the remaining chain through the jump ring and join the two ends with a jump ring to finish.

## DIVING FOR PEARLS (page 55)

### YOU WILL NEED

- Ivory wire mesh ribbon, 40cm (16in)
- Silk or polyester rattail, 40cm (16in)
- Silk beading cord, 45cm (18in) of 0.45mm (0.018in)
- Sterling silver crimp ends, 4mm x 2, 2mm x 2
- Silver-plated spring clasp
- Silver-plated jump ring
- Large knitting needle
- Basic tool kit (see pages 94–95)

SWAROVSKI ELEMENTS

- Crystal Pearl 5810 – White (650) 14mm x 3, 12mm x 4, 8mm x 2
- Round Bead 5000 – Crystal AB (001 AB) 14mm x 2, 12mm x 4, 10mm x 2
- Rondelles 77506 P20 – 6mm x 18

1 Feed the tubular mesh ribbon onto a large knitting needle and then attach the bead cord to the point of the knitting needle with sticky tape. Pull the tubular mesh ribbon off the knitting needle gently to leave the beading cord down the middle of the ribbon. 2 Pick up a 14mm Pearl (5810 14mm 650) on the beading cord, open out the mesh and push the bead through to the middle of the ribbon. 3 Form the mesh into a point shape at one end and feed on a Rondelle (77506 P20 6mm). 4 Open out the mesh and add a 14mm Crystal AB (5000 14mm 001 AB). Repeat the process to add another Rondelle. 5 Continue alternating Crystal Pearls and Swarovski Beads, gradually reducing the size. Repeat on the other side finishing with a crystal Rondelle. 6 Twist the mesh ribbon around the beading cord at each end and feed through a 2mm crimp end. Pull until taut and squeeze the crimp section with snipe-nose pliers to secure. Repeat at the other end. 7 Feed half the rattail through each crimp end. Feed the two tails on each side into the large crimp ends. Secure by squeezing the crimp section with snipe-nose pliers again. 8 Attach a spring clasp with a silver-plated jump ring to one end to finish.

## AUTUMN ELEMENTS (page 66)

### YOU WILL NEED

- Chinese knot beads, 18 x 15mm, burgundy x 2 and copper x 2
- 5 copper metal solid ovals, 18 x 36mm
- Copper chain – three styles, approx. 3, 5 and 6 links per 2.5cm (1in), 50cm (20in) of one and 30cm (12in) of two others
- 20 copper jump rings, 5mm
- 6 copper jump rings, 7mm
- 4 copper headpins, 7cm (2¾in)
- Copper toggle fastening, 10–12mm
- Basic tool kit (see pages 94–95)

SWAROVSKI ELEMENTS

- Cosmic Oval Fancy Stone 4137 – Crystal Red Magma (001 REDM) 22 x 16mm x 1, Crystal Copper (001 COP) 22 x 16mm x 1
- Owlet Sew-on Stone 3231 – Crystal Red Magma (001 REDM) 23 x 14mm x 1, Crystal Copper (001 COP) 23 x 14mm x 1
- Twist Sew-on Stone 3221 – Crystal Red Magma (001 REDM) 18mm x 2, Crystal Copper (001 COP) 18mm x 2

1 Make the Chinese knot beads into bead links using the headpins (see page 99). Trim off the flat end and make a large loop at one end using the widest part of the round-nose pliers' jaws. Insert through the bead, trim wire to 1cm (½in) and make a second loop.
2 Divide some of the chains into 3–5cm (1¼–2in) lengths. Arrange the different elements in three rows, five in the top row and six each in the other two rows. Lay pieces of chain between the elements. 3 Join the different elements to the chain using jump rings (see page 98). Use large jump rings for the oval rings and small jump rings for all the other pieces. The three strands should measure about 35, 39 and 43cm (13¾, 15⅜ and 17in) when finished. You may have to adjust the length of chain at each end of the strands so that the beads don't lie next to one another. 4 Attach a large jump ring to all three strands and then attach a 7cm (2¾in) length of chain. Without twisting the strands, attach another length of chain to the other end. 5 Attach parts of the toggle fastening to each end with small jump rings to finish.

## SHIMMERING SHELL (page 76)

### YOU WILL NEED
- Pressed cotton ball, 2.5cm (1in)
- Turquoise waxed cord, 2mm x 1m (1yd)
- 1 turquoise ceramic bead, 15mm
- Lobster clasp and ring fastening
- 2 silver-plated cord ends
- 2 silver-plated jump rings
- Hotfix tool
- Basic tool kit (see pages 94–5)

SWAROVSKI ELEMENTS
- Flat Backs Hotfix XILION Rose 2028 – a mix of colours in sizes
  SS 5 (1.6mm), SS 9 (2.5mm), SS 12 (3mm) and SS 16 (3.7mm):
  Aquamarine (202), Pacific Opal (390), Blue Zircon (229), Topaz
  (203), Sun (248), Light Topaz (226), Crystal AB (001 AB), Jonquil
  (213), Light Grey Opal (383), Crystal Copper (001 COP)
- Shell Pendant 6723 – Crystal AB (001 AB) 28mm x 1

**1** Apply the Swarovski Flat Backs Hotfix (see page 104) randomly over the pressed cotton ball, spacing out the different colours so that the overall impression is balanced in colour and sizes of crystals. **2** Thread the waxed cord through the Shell Pendant and tie with a reef (square) knot (see page 96). **3** Feed the ends through the crystal-covered bead and tie a reef (square) knot again. **4** Add a ceramic bead and tie the cord in a reef (square) knot again. **5** Trim the cord to the desired length and attach the cord ends (see page 102). **6** Attach a lobster clasp and ring with jump rings to finish.

# Bracelets

## CORDIAL CHARM (page 15)

### YOU WILL NEED
- Spring style bell cone end, 20 x 7mm
  (¾ x ⅜in)
- 4 silver-plated jump rings, 5mm
- 2 silver-plated decorative headpins
- Silver-plated wire, 0.2mm (32swg) and
  0.6mm (24swg)
- Silver-plated lobster claw fastening
- Rattail, 50cm (½yd) each of pink and lilac
- Beading glue
- Basic tool kit (see pages 94–95)

SWAROVSKI ELEMENTS
- Flower Pendant 6744 – Light Rose (223)
  12mm x 2 and Violet (371) 12mm x 2
- Round Bead 5000 – Chrysolite (238) 4mm x 2

> If you can't find decorative headpins, thread a small metal spacer bead on the headpin first.

**1** Holding one end in each hand between finger and thumb, twist each length of rattail until it begins to twist back on itself. Bring the tails together so that it forms a rope and wrap the cut ends with a short length of fine wire to prevent the cord unravelling. **2** Using 0.6mm (24swg) wire, make a wrapped loop through a Flower Pendant (see page 100). Leave a 2mm (⅛in) gap above the wrapping and make a loop that will go over the rattail rope. Secure the loop by wrapping the wire into the gap and then trim neatly. Make a wrapped loop bead link on all the Flower Pendants. **3** Make a plain loop dangle (see page 100) using the decorative headpins and Chrysolite crystals (5000 4mm 238) and attach each to a jump ring. **4** Thread a Flower Pendant then a Bead dangle and another Flower Pendant on each rope. Tie an overhand knot (see page 96) to secure the Beads on each rope about 7.5cm (3in) from the loop end. **5** Check the length of the bracelet, allowing for the bell cone end and fastening. Adjust the length of the ropes if required, rewrapping with fine wire before trimming. **6** Glue the ends into the bell cone end and squeeze the last ring to secure (see page 102). Attach a jump ring through the loop end of the cord then attach a lobster clasp to finish.

## KNOTTED CUFF (page 35)

### YOU WILL NEED

- 20g transparent rainbow seed beads, 2mm
- 15g transparent rainbow teardrops, 4 x 3mm
- 70 opaque white rainbow pony beads, 5mm
- PowerPro braided beading thread in crystal, size D (6lb strength)
- Beading needle, size 10
- Sterling silver bar end fastening with seven holes
- Jewellery glue
- Basic tool kit (see pages 94–95)

SWAROVSKI ELEMENTS
- XILION Bead 5328 – Mint Alabaster (397) 4mm x 90, White Alabaster (281) 4mm x 90, Light Azore (361) 4mm x 90

**1** Fold a 5.5m (6yd) length of beading thread in half. Pass the loop through the centre ring on one bar end and then feed the tails through the loop and pull through to secure. **2** Pick up a mix of beads on the needle to measure exactly 2.5cm (1in), e.g. two 2mm seed beads, a teardrop, a 2mm seed bead, a Mint Alabaster XILION Bead (5328 4mm 397), three 2mm seed beads, a White Alabaster XILION Bead (5328 4mm 281), two 2mm seed beads, a teardrop and a 2mm seed bead. **3** * Pick up a 5mm seed bead and another 2.5cm (1in) mix of Beads. Repeat from * nine times, to make a bead strand about 30cm (12in) long. Take the thread through the centre ring on the other bar end twice and then back through the last seed bead. **4** * Pick up a 2.5cm (1in) mix of Beads (less one seed bead), a 5mm bead and another 2.5cm (1in) mix of Beads. Pass the needle through the next 5mm bead on the first strand. Repeat from * to the last 5mm bead on the previous strand. **5** Add a 2.5cm (1in) mix of Beads and secure the thread to the next ring along.

Repeat from * to work the netting, working along the bar end from ring to ring until you reach the last ring. **6** Secure the thread with half-hitches (see page 96) and a drop of glue. Finish the other side in the same way. **7** To finish, tie the beading in an overhand knot (see page 96) to shape the bracelet.

## OFF THE CUFF (page 46)

### YOU WILL NEED

- Cylinder beads, size 11 (2.2mm), 7g each of transparent rainbow, black metallic matt and grey metallic matt
- Fireline beading thread in smoke, size D
- 3 gunmetal chains in different link sizes
- 3 gunmetal jump rings, 6mm
- 16 gunmetal headpins
- Gunmetal bar end fastening with five holes
- Basic tool kit (see pages 94–95)

SWAROVSKI ELEMENTS
- Briolette Bead 5040 – Jet (280) 6mm x 10
- XILION Bead 5328 – Montana (207) 4mm x 2
- Polygon Bead 5205 – Amethyst (204) 15 x 6mm x 6
- Crystal Pearl 5810 – Powder Rose Pearl (352) 4mm x 4

Make your own gunmetal fastenings by antiquing silver-plated fastenings (see page 101).

**1** To make the beaded ropes, mix the Cylinder Beads and pick up randomly. Using a 1.5m (1½yd) length of beading thread, pick up four cylinder beads and tie in a circle. Pick up two more and circle through the two previous beads and the two just added. Repeat to add two more, then join the two ends by circling through with the needle so that the thread emerges at the opposite side to the tail. **2** Following the instructions for tubular twisted herringbone stitch on page 108, as described in step 2 work two rounds of plain tubular

herringbone stitch and then begin to create the twist. Instead of going down through one bead and up one, go down through two and up one each time and you will find there is no need to step up. Repeat the 'two down one up' until the rope is nearly 20cm (8in) long. Finish the rope as you began with two rounds of plain tubular herringbone stitch and the two-drop ladder stitch. **3** Sew one rope to each of the outer rings on one fastening and one in the middle. Cut three pieces of each chain the same length as the ropes and attach to the same rings with jump rings (see page 98). Plait the ropes once or twice. **4** Make the Polygon Beads (5205 15 x 6mm 204) into bead links (see page 99). Lay a Polygon Bead on the plaiting then attach to the finer chain, cutting away the excess. **5** Continue plaiting and adding the other five Polygon beads as bead links. Sew the plaits to the other bar end and attach the chains with jump rings. **6** Make plain loop headpin dangles (see page 100) with Briolettes (5040 6mm 280), Crystal Pearls (5810 4mm 352) and XILION Beads (5328 4mm 207) and attach to the empty loops on the bar ends and randomly down the bracelet to finish.

## ROCK SOLID (page 75)

### YOU WILL NEED
- 2 antique silver baguette settings, 24 x 8mm
- White marble polymer clay, 40g (1½oz)
- Small rolling pin
- Knitting needles, 5mm (US 8, UK 6)
- Kitchen knife
- 2 fine and 2 heavyweight silver-plated headpins
- Fine elastic clear thread
- Beading glue
- Basic tool kit (see pages 94–95)

SWAROVSKI ELEMENTS
- Princess Baguette Fancy Stone 4547 – Aquamarine (202) 24 x 8mm x 2
- Flat Backs Hotfix XILION Rose 2028 – Aquamarine (202) SS 16 x 45, SS 10 x 60

1 To make clay beads about the same size as the Baguette Fancy Stones (4547 24 x 8mm 202), soften the polymer clay by kneading it with clean hands. 2 Place between the two knitting needles and roll out to a long shape at least 5cm (2in) wide (see page 105). Mark the clay with the headpin 5cm (2in) wide and trim to make a long rectangle shape. Then mark every 1cm (½in) at each side and cut into blocks. 3 Cut each block in half to make fifteen 1 x 2.5cm (½ x 1in) rectangle beads. 4 Gently press the assembled Princess Baguette Fancy Stones on either side of the first clay bead. Turn over and insert a fine headpin through the holes on one Princess Baguette Fancy Stone, through the clay and the second Princess Baguette Fancy Stone. Repeat with the second headpin through the other holes. 5 Peel off the Princess Baguette Fancy Stones and widen the holes with a heavier headpin (or needle). Repeat the process with all the clay beads. 6 Decorate each bead with three large and four small Swarovski Flat Backs Hotfix as shown in the picture on page 75. 7 Place the clay beads on a baking sheet covered in baking parchment or paper. Bake according to the manufacturer's instructions, or for 20 minutes at about 130ºC (250°F / Gas Mark ½). 8 When cooled, string one Baguette Fancy Stone followed by 14 clay beads, then the other Princess Baguette Fancy Stone and the last clay bead. Tie the elastic thread inside the Setting so that the beads sit together and secure the knots with beading glue to finish.

Pick the Swarovski Flat Back Hotfix up with a thin sausage of polymer clay: the crystal sticks to the clay but then drops off when pressed on the bead.

## LUSCIOUS LINKS (page 85)

### YOU WILL NEED
- Silver-plated chain, 20cm (8in) each of two styles one with 10mm links and the other 5mm links
- Silver-plated toggle fastening
- 12 silver-plated jump rings, 6mm
- 10 silver-plated headpins
- Basic tool kit (see pages 94–95)

SWAROVSKI ELEMENTS
- Octagon Two-hole Pendant 6404 – Light Rose (223) 14mm x 2, Tanzanite (539) 14mm x 2, Peridot (214) 14mm x 2
- XILION Bead 5328 – Padparadscha (542) 6mm x 2, Indian Pink (289) 6mm x 2, Tanzanite (539) 6mm x 2, Peridot (214) 6mm x 2, Violet (371) 6mm x 2

1 Make each of the XILION Beads into a bead dangle using the headpins (see page 100). Pick up one Bead on each headpin, bend over at a sharp angle and trim to 7mm (⅜in). Bend the headpin round to create a loop. 2 Divide the larger chain into six two-link sections and the finer chain into six four-link sections. 3 Open the first jump ring and attach to one of the parts of the fastening then loop two pieces of chain on before closing the jump ring (see page 98). 4 Weave the smaller chain through the larger chain and loop onto another open jump ring. Attach to one of the Octagon Two-Hole Pendants. 5 Continue adding the chain between the Two-Hole Pendants and then finish with two pieces of chain and then the fastening. 6 Open the Bead dangle loops then attach two to each piece of the finer chain so that the colours are mixed but there are no colours the same together.

# Rings and Brooches

## CRYSTAL STACKS (page 27)

### YOU WILL NEED

- Cylinder beads, size 11, 3g each of opaque orange and opaque light siam
- Monofilament thread or illusion cord
- Basic tool kit (see pages 94–5)

SWAROVSKI ELEMENTS
- XILION Bead 5328 – approx for each ring:
  Fuchsia (502) 4mm x 10, Rose (209) 4mm x 6, Light Peach (362) 4mm x 4, Fire Opal (237) 4mm x 2, Hyacinth (236) 4mm x 2

Adjust the ring band length before joining it in a tube.

**1** To make the ring band, work in right-angle weave (see page 109) picking up mainly one colour of cylinder bead and just the occasional contrast colour to add interest. **2** Pick up eight cylinder beads and go back through all the beads to make a circle, leaving a 15cm (6in) tail. Take the thread through four beads again to come out at the opposite side to the tail thread. **3** Adding six cylinder beads each time, work a chain of 16 circles in right-angle weave. Work a second column of right-angle weave to make the band and then join the panel into a tube by bringing the two short ends together. **4** Take the needle along the outer beads on each circle on both sides of the ring band to stabilize it. Bring the needle out in the centre of the band. Pick up three XILION Beads and a cylinder bead. Miss the cylinder bead and go back through the XILION Beads. Come out one cylinder bead out on the right-angle weave and make a similar stack but with three cylinder beads,

two XILION Beads and a cylinder bead. Add four of these around the centre stack. **5** Continue adding stacks of different sizes, making shorter stacks with one XILION Bead and a cylinder bead in between previous stacks on the outer ring. Fill in a few stacks in the centre to get the desired effect and sew in the thread ends to finish.

## BEZEL JEWEL (page 65)

### YOU WILL NEED

- 3g raspberry bronze iris Toho seed beads, size 11 (2mm)
- 3g transparent rainbow medium topaz Toho seed beads, size 15 (1mm)
- 3g silver-lined medium amethyst Toho seed beads, size 15 (1mm)
- 2g clear AB Czech charlottes, size 15
- Silver-plated sieve style oval brooch back, 4 x 3cm (1½ x 1¼in)
- S-lon beading thread in brown
- Beading needle, size 13
- Epoxy resin glue
- Basic tool kit (see pages 94–95)

SWAROVSKI ELEMENTS
- Oval Fancy Stone 4127 – Burgundy (515) 30 x 22mm x 1
- Oval Fancy Stone 4120 – Smoked Topaz (220) 14 x 10mm x 1, Topaz (203) 14 x 10mm x 1, Padparadscha (542) 14 x 10mm x 1
- Square Fancy Stone 4470 – Smoked Topaz (220) 10mm x 1, Padparadscha (542) 10mm x 1, Burgundy (515) 10mm x 1, Smoky Quartz (225) 10mm x 1
- Rivoli Chaton 1122 – Fuchsia (F 502) 12mm x 2

To begin a bezel on any size of stone, string enough seed beads in an even number, to fit around the circumference and tie in a circle (see page 107).

**1** To make the bezel, string the required number of size 11 raspberry bronze iris seed beads and tie in a circle (see tip). Pass the needle through two seed beads to hide the knot. **2** * Pick up a raspberry bronze iris seed bead, miss a bead and take the needle through the next seed bead. Continue from * to complete the round. **3** Step up through the last seed bead in the ring and the first one added in the last round. Work two rounds with size 15 amethyst seed beads and then pull the thread taut to create a tubular piece of beading. Finish that side with a round of size 15 Czech charlottes. **4** Take the needle through the beads to the other edge. Fit the large Oval Fancy Stone (4127 30 x 22mm 515) in the bezel. Repeat from * to enclose the stone. Pull the thread taut and sew in the ends. **5** Stitch a bezel around each stone using size 15 topaz seed beads on brown or yellow stones and size 15 amethyst seed beads on pink toned stones. **6** Arrange the smaller crystals around the large Oval Fancy Stone as shown in the picture on page 65. Sew the bezels together one by one where they touch. **7** To finish attach a large oval brooch back to the back of the central stone with epoxy resin or by stitching.

## FRUITY CLUSTER (page 86)

### YOU WILL NEED
- 24 silver-plated headpins
- Silver-plated ring base with eight loops
- Basic tool kit (see pages 94–95)

SWAROVSKI ELEMENTS
- Round Bead 5000 – Jonquil (213) 6mm x 1, Tanzanite (539) 6mm x 1, Blue Zircon (229) 6mm x 1, Peridot (214) 6mm x 1, Padparadscha (542) 6mm x 1, Indian Pink (289) 6mm x 1, Chrysolite (238) 6mm x 1, Aquamarine (202) 6mm x 1
- Cube Bead 5601 – Light Topaz (226) 4mm x 2, Amethyst (204) 4mm x 2, Light Rose (223) 4mm x 2, Rose (209) 4mm x 2
- Briolette Bead 5040 – Peridot (214) 6mm x 2, Amethyst (204) 6mm x 2, Topaz (203) 6mm x 2, Aquamarine (202) 6mm x 2

Don't make the loops on the dangles too small or it will be difficult to add the dangles to the ring base as it becomes fuller.

**1** Make each of the SWAROVSKI ELEMENTS into a bead dangle using the headpins (see page 100). Pick up one Swarovski Bead on each headpin, bend over at a sharp angle and trim to 7mm (⅜in). Bend the headpin round to create a loop. **2** Open each loop in turn and attach to the ring. Work out from the centre loops, adding three headpin dangles to each loop. **3** Mix the colours and shapes so that the dark shades are not all in one place.

# Earrings

## BUTTERFLY KISSES (page 16)

### YOU WILL NEED
- Purple waxed cord 1m (1yd) of 1mm
- 12 silver-plated headpins
- 2 silver-plated jump rings
- 2 silver-plated earring wires
- Tapestry needle
- Beading glue
- Basic tool kit (see pages 94–95)

SWAROVSKI ELEMENTS
- Butterfly Pendant 6754 – Violet (371) 18mm x 2
- Round Bead 5000 – Violet (371) 6mm x 4, Chrysolite (238) 6mm x 4, Padparadscha (542) 6mm x 4
- Marguerite Lochrose 3700 – Peridot (214) 6mm x 12

**1** Cut the waxed cord in half then feed the end through the hole in the Pendant (6754 18mm 371) twice to form two loops that fit over three fingers. **2** Move round so that one tail is level with the bottom of the butterfly and the other is longer. **3** Wrap the long tail around the loops nine times. Thread onto a needle and feed down through the wrapping. Pull the needle with the cord through. **4** Ease the wrapping away from the butterfly slightly, apply glue and ease back down. **5** Pick up a Swarovski Bead 5000 and a Marguerite Lochrose (3700 6mm 214) on a headpin and make a bead dangle (see page 100). Repeat with all the crystals. **6** Add three dangles around all cords on one side of the earring and three on the other side. **7** Attach a jump ring over the cords at the top of the earring and add an earring wire (see page 99). Make a second earring to match.

## ICICLE FRINGE (page 37)

### YOU WILL NEED

- 15g transparent rainbow seed beads, 2mm
- Fine cord thread in white
- Big-eye needle, 12cm (4¾in)
- 2 sterling silver earring findings
- Silver-plated wire, 0.6mm (24swg)
- Sterling silver bar end fastening with five holes
- Basic tool kit (see pages 94–95)

SWAROVSKI ELEMENTS
- XILION Bead 5328 – Light Azore (361) 4mm x 40, Pacific Opal (390) 4mm x 34

An extra long beading needle lets you pick up all the beads for the fringe in one go.

**1** Cut five 50cm (20in) lengths of thread, fold each in half and attach with a lark's head knot (see page 96) to the rings on one bar end. **2** Tape the fastening to the work surface. Use the big-eye needle to thread a seed bead and a Light Azore XILION Bead (5328 4mm 361) to each pair of threads. **3** Separate the threads and add a Pacific Opal XILION Bead (5328 4mm 390) and a seed bead to every second thread. **4** On the alternate threads pick up a seed bead and take the needle through the adjacent XILION Bead and pick up another seed bead. **5** Thread a light azore XILION Bead (5328 4mm 361) on each pair of threads again. Separate the threads again and pick up 15 seed beads, a light azore XILION Bead, 20 seed beads, a Pacific Opal XILION Bead (5328 4mm 390) and a seed bead on the first thread. Miss the last seed bead and take the needle back through all the seed beads. Leave the tail. **6** Add the same fringe strand to each thread so that there are two threads coming out below each Light Azore XILION Bead (5328 4mm 361). Pull up the beads so that they are taut and sitting snugly together. **7** Thread a pair of threads into a small beading needle and work a half-hitch knot (see page 96) between the seed bead strands and the Light Azore XILION Beads. Pull tight and feed the thread through the beads above. Trim the end. Repeat with each pair of tails. Make a second earring to match. **8** Make two bead links (see page 99) using a seed bead, a Pacific Opal XILION Bead (5328 4mm 390) and a seed bead. Turn the loops so that they are facing in different directions. Attach one end of the bead link to the top of the bar end and the other end to the earring finding on each earring to finish.

## IN THE LOOP (page 47)

### YOU WILL NEED

- 2 gunmetal loop earring findings, 4cm (1½in)
- Gunmetal chain in two styles, 30cm (12in) of each
- 2 gunmetal jump rings, 6mm
- 8 gunmetal headpins
- 2 gunmetal earring wires
- Basic tool kit (see pages 94–95)

SWAROVSKI ELEMENTS
- XILION Bead 5328 – Crystal Vitrail Medium (001 VM) 4mm x 62
- Polygon Bead 5205 – Jet (280) 15 x 6mm x 8

**1** Open the earring loop finding and thread on the XILION Beads (5328 4mm 001 VM) to fill then close the loop. **2** Open a jump ring (see page 98). Cut four graduated lengths of chain at least 4cm (1½in) long and feed two onto the jump ring. **3** Feed the jump ring through the loop at the top of the finding and add two more lengths to the other side. Close the jump ring. **4** Make bead dangles with a plain loop (see page 100) using the Polygon Beads (5205 15 x 6mm 280). **5** Attach one bead dangle to the bottom of each length of chain. **6** Fit the earring wires to the jump ring (see page 99). Drape two chains down one side of the loop and two down the other to finish.

## PEARL DROPS (page 57)

### YOU WILL NEED
- Silver-plated hammered square rings, 25mm x 2
- Silver-plated headpins x 2
- Silver-plated eyepins x 2
- Silver-plated earring wires
- Basic tool kit (see pages 94–95)

SWAROVSKI ELEMENTS
- Crystal Pearls 5810 – White (650)
  14mm x 2, 10mm x 2
- Round Bead 5000 – Crystal AB (001 AB)
  10mm x 2, 8mm x 2
- Swarovski Rondelles 77506 P20 – 6mm x 4
- XILION Bead 5238 – Crystal AB (001 AB)
  3mm x 2

**1** Pick up a 3mm XILION Bead (5238 3mm 001 AB), a 14mm pearl (5810 14mm 650), a Rondelle (77506 P20) and a 10mm Round Bead (5000 10mm 001 AB) on each headpin. **2** Using snipe-nose pliers, bend the headpin over after the large crystal. Trim to 1cm (½in) and form into a loop with round-nose pliers (see page 99). **3** On each eyepin pick up an 8mm Round Bead (5000 8mm 001 AB), a Rondelle (77506 P20) and a 10mm Crystal Pearl (5810 10mm 650). Trim in the same way as the headpin and make a loop on each eyepin. **4** Open the loops on the headpins and attach to the hammered square rings. **5** Open the large loops on the eyepins and attach to the other side of the rings. **6** Attach earring wires to the small loop on each earring to finish.

## STARFISH SPARKLES (page 77)

### YOU WILL NEED
- 2 sterling silver earring findings with two or three holes
- Sterling silver chain, 20cm (8in)
- 12 sterling silver jump rings, 5mm
- Hotfix tool (see page 104)
- Basic tool kit (see pages 94–95)

SWAROVSKI ELEMENTS
- Starfish Pendant 6721 – Aquamarine (202)
  16mm x 2 and Crystal AB (001 AB)
  16mm x 2
- Flat Backs Hotfix XILION Rose 2028 –
  Aquamarine (202) SS 6 x 2, SS 10 x 2

**1** Using a hotfix tool embellish the earring findings with Swarovski Flat Back Hotfix (see page 104). The design of your particular findings will dictate where to place the crystals. If the finding has three holes, cover the middle hole with a crystal. **2** Cut the chain into two 3cm (1¼in) lengths and two 5cm (2in) lengths. **3** Attach a jump ring (see page 98) to each of the Starfish Pendants then use a second jump ring to attach the AB Pendants (6721 16mm 001 AB) to the shorter chains and the Aquamarine Pendants (6721 16mm 202) to the longer lengths of chain. **4** Lay the earring findings down and attach the aquamarine pendant chains to the outer holes in each finding with jump rings. **5** To finish, attach the Crystal AB pieces of chain to the inner holes in the earring finding, making sure that the coated side is at the back when the earrings are worn.

## RUBY DANGLES (page 87)

### YOU WILL NEED
- 2 silver-plated earring wires,
- 4 silver-plated jump rings
- 4 silver-plated headpins
- Basic tool kit (see pages 94–95)

SWAROVSKI ELEMENTS
- Round Bead 5000 – Jonquil (213) 2mm x 2, 4mm x 2, Tanzanite (539) 4mm x 4
- Spacer Bead 5305 – Peridot (214) 5mm x 4
- Octagon Two-Hole Pendant 6404 – Ruby (501) 14mm x 2

**1** Pick up a 4mm Jonquil Bead (5000 4mm 213), a Peridot Spacer Bead (5305 5mm 214), a Tanzanite Round Bead (5000 4mm 539) and another Spacer Bead on a headpin. Bend the tail at a sharp angle close to the last bead, trim to 7mm (⅜in) and make a loop with round-nose pliers (see page 100). **2** Trim the head off another headpin and make an eyepin loop on one end (see page 99). **3** Pick up a Spacer Bead, a Tanzanite Round Bead, a Spacer Bead and a 2mm Jonquil Round Bead (5000 2mm 213). Make a loop after the last bead as you did with the headpin dangle. **4** Open two jump rings (see page 98) and insert one into a hole in a Ruby Octagon Two-Hole Pendant (6404 14mm 501). Attach the bead dangle and close the ring. **5** Attach the bead link to the other side of the Two-Hole Pendant. **6** Attach an earring wire to the loop at the top of the bead link (see page 99). **7** Make a second earring to match.

# Accessories

## GLISTENING DEMOISELLE
(page 17)

### YOU WILL NEED
- 2g silver seed beads, size 15 charlottes
- Silver-plated wire, 0.6mm (26swg) and 0.315mm (30swg)
- Pink tubular mesh metallic ribbon, 50cm (½yd) of 6mm
- Sewing thread and needle
- Bamboo skewer
- Hair clip or comb
- Basic tool kit (see pages 94–95)

SWAROVSKI ELEMENTS
- Modular Bead 5150 – Tanzanite (539) 11 x 6mm x 1
- Round Bead 5000 – Crystal AB (001 AB) 2mm x 10, Peridot (214) 2mm x 10, Tanzanite (539) 2mm x 10, Amethyst (204) 2mm x 10
- Round Bead 5000 – Peridot (214) 2mm x 3, 3mm x 3, 4mm x 3, 6mm x 3, 7mm x 3

**1** Bend a 60cm (24in) length of 0.6mm (26swg) silver-plated wire in half and open out again. Shape the wire over the head of snipe-nose pliers to make a 4.5cm (1¾in) wing to both sides. **2** Cross the wires over and fold back level with the previous wings so that you can create the second set of wings. **3** Wrap the tails around the centre once, twist the ends together and trim neatly. **4** Cut four 12cm (4¾in) lengths of mesh ribbon. Feed one piece onto a wing, twist at the tip of the wing, open out the end and double back to make a second layer. Repeat with each wing and sew neatly in position. **5** On 0.315mm (30swg) silver-plated wire, * pick up four silver seed beads and six mixed 2mm Swarovski Beads and the odd silver seed bead. Repeat from * seven times and finish with four silver seed beads. **6** To create the body: leaving a 10cm (4in) tail at each end, wrap the wire around a bamboo skewer a few times and then wrap the beads, finishing with a few turns of the wire. **7** Wrap a 30cm (12in) length of 0.6mm (26swg) wire around the Modular Bead (5150

11 x 6mm 539) a few times, feed the spiral bead you've made on to the wires then pick up the Peridot Beads in size order starting with the 7mm Swarovski Beads (5000 7mm 214) and finishing with the 2mm Beads (5000 2mm 214). **8** Trim to 5mm (¼in) and form a tiny loop on the end. Use the wire tails to attach the wings and then to sew the dragonfly onto a hair clip.

## FLORAL TRESSES (page 26)

### YOU WILL NEED
- Cylinder beads, size 11, 3g each of opaque orange and opaque light siam
- Bright orange or bright pink hair bauble elastic
- Basic tool kit (see pages 94–95)

SWAROVSKI ELEMENTS
- XILION Bead 5328 – Rose (209) 4mm x 32, Light Peach (362) 4mm x 26, Fire Opal (237) 4mm x 2, Hyacinth (236) 4mm x 2, Dark Red Coral (396) 6mm x 1

**1** To make the bead tube, work in right-angle weave (see page 109) picking up colours in a random order using more of the rose XILION Beads (5328 4mm 209) than Light Peach (5328 4mm 362) and just the occasional Fire Opal (5328 4mm 237) and hyacinth (5328 4mm 236) to add interest. **2** Pick up a cylinder bead and a XILION Bead four times. Work a chain of seven circles in right-angle weave following the steps in the bracelet project on page 20 but using 4mm XILION Beads and cylinder beads. Then work three columns to make a panel three

circles wide and seven circles long with the thread coming out at the top XILION Bead at one side. **3** Wrap the panel around the hair bauble elastic and join the sides together by adding XILION Beads and cylinder beads to continue the pattern and complete the tube. **4** Sew through the elastic to secure the metal section of the bauble inside the right-angle weave tube and sew in the thread ends. **5** For the flower motif, string four Rose XILION Beads (5328 4mm 209) and go through all again to make a circle. Follow the diagram on page 126 to complete the flower shape. **6** Take the thread into the outer edge of the centre four Rose XILION Beads. Pick up a light siam cylinder bead, a Dark Red Coral XILION Bead (5328 6mm 396) and a light siam cylinder bead and sew diagonally over the Rose XILION Beads. Bring the needle back through one of the end cylinder beads, pick up eight red cylinder beads and go through the single cylinder bead at the other end. **7** Add eight cylinder beads on the other side then sew onto the hair bauble to finish.

## LATTICE CHARM (page 36)

### YOU WILL NEED
- 5g transparent rainbow seed beads, 2mm
- Large round white or aqua bead, 2.5mm
- Clear monofilament thread or illusion cord, 2m (2¼yd) of 0.3mm (0.012in)
- Beading needle, size 10
- Bag charm clip
- Silver-plated chain, 5cm (2in)
- 2 silver-plated jump rings
- Silver-plated headpin, 5cm (2in)
- Short piece of silver-plated wire, 0.6mm (24swg)
- Basic tool kit (see pages 94–95)

SWAROVSKI ELEMENTS
- XILION Bead 5328 – Mint Alabaster (397) 4mm x 50
- Round Bead 5000 – Crystal AB (001 AB) 8mm x 2

**1** Pick up ten seed beads on the thread, take the needle back through the beads again to make a circle and tie a reef (square) knot (see page 96). **2** Pick up a seed bead and go through the next two seed beads. Repeat four times and pass the needle through the first seed bead added again (see page 111). **3** On the next round, * pick up one seed bead, a XILION Bead (5328 4mm 397) and one seed bead and take the needle through the next seed bead added in the last round. Repeat from * all the way round, then step up through one seed bead and a XILION Bead. **4** On the next round add one seed bead, a XILION Bead and a seed bead between the XILION Beads from the last round and step up through a seed bead and a XILION Bead. **5** Work two rounds with two seed beads either side of the XILION Beads, then three rounds with three seed beads. Insert the large bead into the netting and then work the other side, reducing the seed beads to match the other side (so work two rounds with two seed beads and one round with one seed bead). **6** On the next round pick up three seed beads between every second XILION Bead in the previous round

then on the next round pick up two seed beads between the centre seed beads in the previous round. **7** Pull up to tighten the beads and go back through the last ten seed beads and secure the thread with one or two half-hitches (see page 96). **8** Pick up a Mint Alabaster XILION Bead (5328 4mm 397), a Round Bead (5000 8mm 001 AB), the net bead and another Round Bead. Form a plain loop on the end (see page 100). **9** Make a Mint Alabaster XILION Bead (5328 4mm 397) and two seed beads into a bead link (see page 99) and insert in the middle of a piece of chain. To finish, attach the chain to the bead charm and to the bag charm clip using a jump ring (see page 98).

## CRYSTAL CLUSTERS (page 56)

### YOU WILL NEED

- Ivory silk georgette, 1m (1yd) wide x 20cm (8in)
- Silver-plated wire, 0.2mm (36swg)
- Needle and ivory sewing thread
- Glue gun or epoxy resin
- Basic tool kit (see pages 94–95)

SWAROVSKI ELEMENTS
- XILION Bead 5328 – Crystal Vitrail Medium (001 VM) 3mm x 30; Crystal AB (001 AB) 3mm x 25
- Crystal Pearl 5810 – White (650) 8mm x 5

**1** Tear a 4.5cm (1¾in) strip from the georgette. If the piece was originally cut off the roll you will need to tear across to get the first frayed edge. Cut straight across the grain to make five 20cm (8in) lengths and fray each end slightly. **2** Fold the first strip almost in half till the frayed edges are layered and sew running stitches along the fold. Pull the thread to gather and sew the ends together to make a circular shape. Make five the same. **3** Cut five 10cm (4in) lengths of fine wire, pick up a Crystal Pearl (5810 8mm 650) on each, fold the wire down each side and twist the Crystal Pearl between finger and thumb to secure. **4** Working off the reel, pick up six 3mm Vitrail Medium XILION Beads (5328 3mm 001 VM). Fold the wire over a XILION Bead 5cm (2in) from the tail end and twist 2.5cm (1in) to secure. Repeat with each XILION Bead in turn. Make five the same. **5** Repeat with five AB XILION Beads (5328 3mm 001 AB). Make five the same. **6** Wrap the AB wire stems around the pearl stems and twist the wires together at the back. Feed the tail through the centre of the georgette puffs, coil around at the back and trim. **7** Secure the beady puffs onto the comb with a glue gun or epoxy resin to finish.

## COSMIC CORDS (page 67)

### YOU WILL NEED

- Brown rattail, 2mm x 50cm (½yd)
- 2 copper spacers, 10mm with a 5mm hole
- Copper bell cone end, 6 x 8mm (¼ x ⅜in)
- Copper headpin
- Copper lobster claw clasp, 19mm
- Fine wire, 0.2mm (36swg)
- Beading glue
- Basic tool kit (see pages 94–95)

SWAROVSKI ELEMENTS
- Cosmic Ring Fancy Stone 4139 – Crystal Volcano (001 VOL) 20mm x 1, Crystal Golden Shadow (001 GSHA) 30mm x 1

**1** Cut the rattail in half and loop one piece round each cosmic ring. Trim the ends at an angle and thread each pair through a copper spacer. **2** Hold one end of the rattail in each hand and twist in opposite directions between your finger and thumb until the rattail begins to twist back on itself to create a thick cord. Keep twisting to the end and wrap with a short piece of fine wire to secure. **3** Finish the other ring in the same way. **4** Hold the two ropes together so that the rings are staggered and wrap wire again around the ropes about 8cm (3in) from the larger ring. Trim the excess cord. **5** Insert the headpin into the copper bell cone end and make a small wrapped loop using round-nose pliers (see page 100). **6** Attach the lobster clasp with a jump ring to finish.

When using bell cone ends (see page 102), the design looks better and is more secure if you have a tight fit around the rope.

# BEAD DETAILS

The details of specific beads (non Swarovski ELEMENTS) are listed below. Any beads without a shop reference are either fashion beads without precise details or basic beads, generally available from your local bead shop. See page 125 for Suppliers.

## BRIGHT *and* BOLD

**Rocky Road Bangle** (page 19)
2.6mm pearlized seed beads – 14 068 18 (pale red) and
  14 068 34 (pale orange): Rayher Hobby
**Crochet and Cubes** (page 25)
Crochet beads: Edinburgh Bead Shop
**Floral Tresses** (page 26) and **Crystal Stacks** (page 27)
Delicas – AB 161 (opaque orange) and AB 159 (opaque light
  siam): Edinburgh Bead Shop

## COOL *and* CHIC

**Knotted Cuff** (page 35)
2mm seed beads – 5500 250 (transparent rainbow); 4 x 3mm
  teardrops – 5524 250 (transparent rainbow); 5mm pony
  beads – 5523 402 (opaque white rainbow): Knorr Prandell
**Icicle Fringe** (page 37)
2mm seed beads – 5500 250 (transparent rainbow):
  Knorr Prandell

## DARK *and* DANGEROUS

**Off the Cuff** (page 46)
Cylinder beads – 14 751 576 (black metallic matt), 14 751 572
  (grey metallic matt) and 14 755 364 (transparent rainbow):
  Rayher Hobby

## RICH *and* WARM

**Cabochon Ring** (page 59)
Size 11 (2mm) Toho hexagon – 221 (bronze); size 15 (1mm)
  Toho seed beads – 167F (transparent frosted rainbow medium
  topaz), 423F (transparent frosted smoky topaz), 034 (silver-
  lined smoked topaz), 553 (galvanized pink/lilac): E-Beads Ltd
Size 11 (2mm) Toho seed beads – 319A (topaz rose gold lustre):
  Out on a Whim
Size 15 gold Czech charlottes: Edinburgh Bead Shop
**Bezel Jewel** (page 65)
Size 11 (2mm) Toho seed beads – 460A (raspberry bronze
  iris); size 15 (1mm) Toho seed beads – 162B (transparent
  rainbow medium topaz), 26B (silver-lined medium
  amethyst): E-Beads Ltd
Size 15 (1mm) clear AB Czech charlottes: Edinburgh Bead Shop
**Autumn Elements** (page 66)
Chinese knot beads: Edinburgh Bead Shop

## SEA *and* SHORE

**Seahorse Necklace** (page 69)
Silver seahorse charm: Alchemia Studio

# SUPPLIERS

## UK and Europe

### E-Beads Ltd
Unit TR1-2 Trowbray House
108 Weston Street
London
SE1 3QB
Tel: 0207 367 62 17
Email: via website
UK: www.e-beads.co.uk
EU: www.i-beads.eu
DE: www.i-perlen.de
FR: www.i-perles.fr
AT: www.iperlen.at
BE: www.i-perles.be

### Alchemia Studio
99 Market Street
St Andrews
KY16 9NX
Tel: 01334 475588
Email: via website
www.alchemia.co.uk

### Bead Crazy
55 George Street
Perth
PH1 5LB
Tel: 01738442288
Email: info@beadcrazy.co.uk
www.beadcrazy.co.uk

### Edinburgh Bead Shop
6 Dean Park Street
Stockbridge
Edinburgh
EH4 1JW
Tel: 0131 343 3222
Email: info@beadshopedinburgh.co.uk
www.beadshopscotland.co.uk

### Jencel
30 Lees Hall Avenue
Sheffield
S8 9JE
Tel: 0114 250 9565
Email: celia@jencel.co.uk
www.jencel.co.uk

### Jilly Beads
1 Anstable Road
Morecambe
LA4 6TG
Tel: 01524 412728
Email: query@jillybeads.co.uk
www.jillybeads.co.uk

### Knorr Prandell
Perivale-Gütermann Ltd
Bullsbrook Road
Hayes, Middlesex
UB4 0JR
Tel: 0208 589 1624
Email: perivale@guetermann.com
www.guetermann.com

### Rayher Hobby
Fockestrasse 15
88471 Laupeim
Germany
Tel: 07392 70050
Email: info@rayher-hobby.de
www.rayher-hobby.de/en

### The Bead Shop (Nottingham)
7 Market Street
Nottingham
NG1 6HY
Tel: 0115 9588903
Email: info@mailorderbeads.co.uk
www.mailorderbeads.co.uk

### The Scientific Wire Company
18 Raven Road
London E18 1HW
Tel: 0208 505 0002
www. wires.co.uk

## USA

### Bead It!
590 Farrington Highway
Kapolei
HI 96707
Tel: 808 674 1192
Email: kapoleistore@beads.com
www.ibeads.com

### Firemountain Gems
1 Firemountain Way
Grants Pass
OR 97526-2373
Tel: 800 423 2319
Email: questions@firemtn.com
www.firemountain.com

### Out on a Whim
121 E. Eotali Avenue
Cotati
CA 94931
Tel: 800 232 3111
Email: via website
www.whimbeads.com

### The Beadin' Path
15 Main Street
Freeport
ME 04032
Tel: 207 865 4785
Email: beads@beadinpath.com
www.beadinpath.com

## SWAROVSKI CRYSTALLIZED™ Stores

Innovative, interactive concept stores
'A unique shopping experience'
www.swarovski-crystallized.com

24 Great Marlborough Street
(Opposite Liberty)
London
W1F 7HU
Tel: 0207 434 3444
Email: customerservice.uk@
crystallized.com

499 Broadway
(Between Spring Street and Broome Street)
New York City
NY 10012
USA
Tel: 800 873 7578
Email: customerservice.us@
crystallized.com

522 Huai Hai Road Central
(Between Yan Dang Road and Chengdu Road South)
Shanghai
Lu Wan District
PRC 200020
China
Tel: 86 21 5382 8508
Email: customerservice.cn@crystallized.com

Kärntner Straße 24
1010 Wien
Austria
Tel: 01 324 0000
Email: swarovski.wien@swarovski.com

Kristallweltenstraße 1
6112 Wattens
Austria
Tel: 05224 51080
Email: customer.relations.sts@
swarovski.com

Herzog-Friedrich-Straße 39
6020 Innsbruck
Austria
Tel: 0573 100
Email: swarovski.innsbruck@
swarovski.com

# ABOUT THE AUTHOR

Dorothy Wood is a talented and prolific beader, craft maker and author. Since completing a course in Advanced Embroidery and Textiles at Goldsmith's College, London, she has written over 20 craft books, and contributed to many others, on all kinds of subjects. This is Dorothy's ninth book for David & Charles, her previous books including the best-selling *Simple Glass Beading*, *Ultimate Necklace Maker* and *The Beader's Bible*. She also contributes to several well-known craft magazines, including *Make Jewellery*, *Knit Today*, *Quick Cards*, and *Cardmaking & Papercrafts*. Dorothy can be contacted via her website at **www.dorothywood.co.uk**

# ACKNOWLEDGMENTS

**The publishers:** Thanks to SWAROVSKI ELEMENTS for their support and for providing many of the beautiful crystals used, and in particular Laura Brocklebank, Account Manager for SWAROVSKI ELEMENTS, for her guidance and advice throughout the project. Thanks are also owed to E-Beads Limited. Visit www.e-beads.co.uk for an excellent online shopping experience, browsable in English, French and German.

**Dorothy Wood:** It has been a pleasure designing the projects for this book using stunning beads from the SWAROVSKI ELEMENTS range and I would like to also thank E-Beads, Rayher Hobby and Knorr Prandell who were so generous supplying additional crystals, beads and materials for many of the projects. Thanks to Jennifer Fox-Proverbs for giving me the opportunity to write this book, to Ame Verso for editing my manuscript so adeptly and to the team at David & Charles for their support and expertise putting the book together. Thanks also to Sian Irvine and Ally Stuart for the gorgeous photography which shows the projects so beautifully; and long overdue thanks to my husband, David, for his unfailing support.

# DIAGRAMS

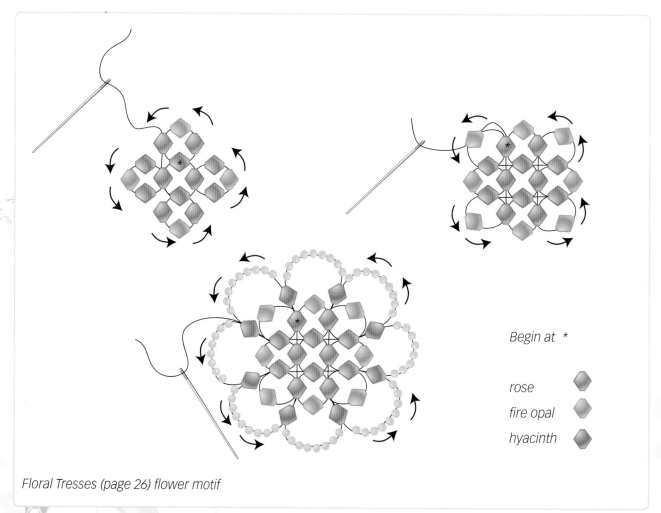

Begin at *

rose

fire opal

hyacinth

*Floral Tresses (page 26) flower motif*

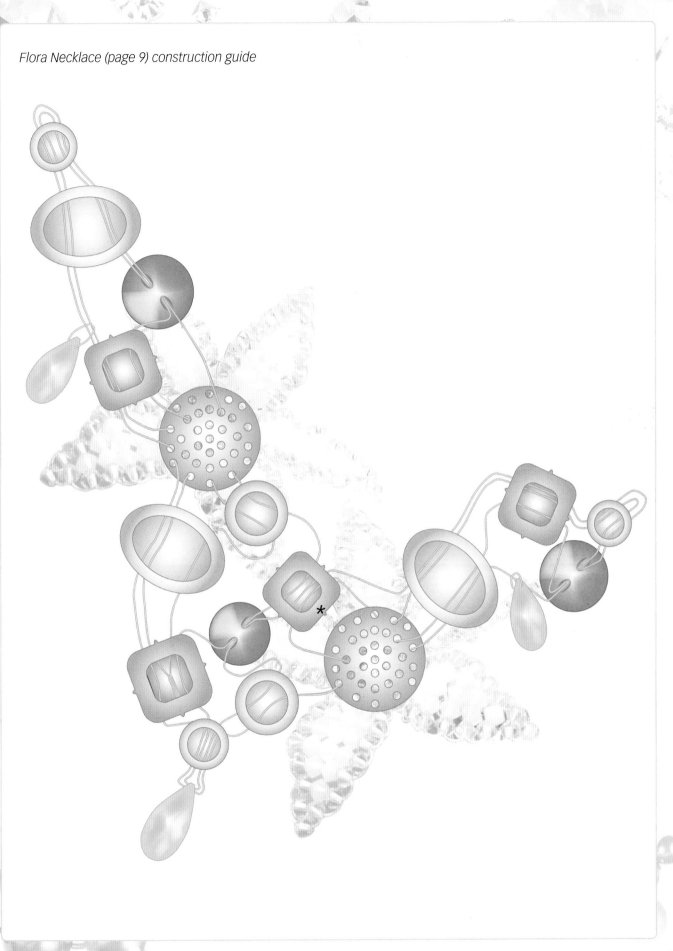

# INDEX